21天攻克 PET 核心词汇

张 羽　王孟霞 / 编著

电子工業出版社
Publishing House of Electronics Industry
北京·BEIJING

图书在版编目（CIP）数据

21 天攻克 PET 核心词汇 / 张羽，王孟霞编著 . —北京：电子工业出版社，2022.7

ISBN 978-7-121-43904-9

Ⅰ . ① 2… Ⅱ . ①张… ②王… Ⅲ . ①英语水平考试－词汇－自学参考资料 Ⅳ . ① H319.34

中国版本图书馆 CIP 数据核字（2022）第 118221 号

责任编辑：曲安琪

印　　刷：北京市大天乐投资管理有限公司

装　　订：北京市大天乐投资管理有限公司

出版发行：电子工业出版社

　　　　　北京市海淀区万寿路 173 信箱　邮编　100036

开　　本：787×1 092　1/16　印张：10.25　字数：324 千字

版　　次：2022 年 7 月第 1 版

印　　次：2022 年 7 月第 1 次印刷

定　　价：48.00 元

凡所购买电子工业出版社图书有缺损问题，请向购买书店调换。若书店售缺，请与本社发行部联系，联系及邮购电话：（010）88254888，88258888。

质量投诉请发邮件至 zlts@phei.com.cn，盗版侵权举报请发邮件至 dbqq@phei.com.cn。

本书咨询联系方式：（010）88254690，qaq@phei.com.cn。

Foreword

剑桥英语五级证书考试（MSE）是英国剑桥大学考试委员会专为母语为非英语的人士所设计的英语五级系列考试，侧重从英语听、说、读、写等四个方面考查考生英语能力。剑桥英语考试中的第二级初级英语考试（PET）重点考查考生用英语处理日常事务及与讲英语的人士进行交流的能力。

编著者以最新的 PET 词汇表为基础，根据官方的主题词汇列表及 PET 考试中的高频话题，甄选核心词汇 1300+ 个，将所有词汇分成 21 个贴合考试且与青少年日常生活密切相关的主题。一天学习一个主题，让考生对核心词汇的发音、含义、拼写、应用等进行高效记忆，21 天攻克 PET 核心词汇。

每个主题下设有核心词汇列表、"进阶加油站"、词汇练习题和"中英互译自测"四大板块。其中，根据核心词汇在 PET 考试中的出现频率和重要程度，核心词汇列表分为基础词汇（KET 阶段已掌握的词汇）列表和重点词汇（PET 阶段需掌握的词汇）列表，重难点突出，帮助考生精准备考；"进阶加油站"板块包括词汇扩展、词汇辨析、高频短语、语法知识等，帮助考生快速扩大词汇量，提升在具体语境中运用词汇的能力；词汇练习题的类型多样，包括匹配题、选择题、填空题和 PET 模拟题，方便考生全面检测学习效果，熟练掌握词汇考点。"中英互译自测"板块帮助考生夯实单词的音、形、义对应。

编著者建议考生按照"学前测评—重点记忆—练习检测—复习巩固"的顺序完成各主题的核心词汇学习。对于基础词汇，要做到烂熟于心；对于重点词汇，要做到会听、会读、会写；对于"进阶加油站"板块，要多多积累语用知识。

☞ **学前测评**：快速浏览核心词汇列表，同时用手或纸遮住词汇含义，对自己的词汇量进行测评，标记出不熟悉或不认识的词汇。

☞ **重点记忆**：集中力量攻克不熟悉或不认识的词汇，学习"进阶加油站"的相应知识。

☞ **练习检测**：认真完成词汇练习题，加深词汇记忆，提升英语综合能力。

☞ **复习巩固**：利用核心词汇列表中的"默写"一栏和"中英互译自测"板块查漏补缺。

希望本书能够陪伴考生一起成长，也真诚欢迎考生在使用本书的过程中提出宝贵的意见与建议。

编著者
2022 年 7 月

CONTENTS

Day ❶ *Education* 教育

VOCABULARY

✅ 基础词汇

词 汇	词 义		默 写
advanced /əd'vɑːnst/	*adj.*	高级的；高等的	
beginner /bɪ'gɪnə(r)/	*n.*	初学者	
biology /baɪ'ɒlədʒi/	*n.*	生物学	
blackboard /'blækbɔːd/	*n.*	黑板	
board /bɔːd/	*n.*	板	
bookshelf /'bʊkʃelf/	*n.*	书架	
chemistry /'kemɪstri/	*n.*	化学	
coach /kəʊtʃ/	*n.*	教练；私人教师	
course /kɔːs/	*n.*	课程	
dictionary /'dɪkʃənri/	*n.*	词典；字典	
geography /dʒi'ɒgrəfi/	*n.*	地理（学）	
history /'hɪstri/	*n.*	历史	
information /ˌɪnfə'meɪʃn/	*n.*	信息；消息	
instruction /ɪn'strʌkʃn/	*n.*	指示；命令；用法说明	
level /'levl/	*n.*	水平；标准	
library /'laɪbrəri/	*n.*	图书馆	
mark /mɑːk/	*n.*	分数；标记；污点	
mathematics /ˌmæθə'mætɪks/	*n.*	数学	
note /nəʊt/	*n.*	笔记；便条	

physics /ˈfɪzɪks/	*n.*	物理学
practice /ˈpræktɪs/	*n.*	实践；惯例；习惯；练习
pupil /ˈpjuːpl/	*n.*	学生；（尤指）小学生
science /ˈsaɪəns/	*n.*	科学
subject /ˈsʌbdʒɪkt/	*n.*	学科
term /tɜːm/	*n.*	学期；术语
test /test/	*n.*	测验；考查
text /tekst/	*n.*	课本；文章
textbook /ˈtekstbʊk/	*n.*	教科书；课本
university /ˌjuːnɪˈvɜːsəti/	*n.*	大学
writing /ˈraɪtɪŋ/	*n.*	书写
written /ˈrɪtn/	*adj.*	书面的

✓ 重点词汇

词汇	词义	默写
absent /ˈæbsənt/	*adj.* 缺席	
achieve /əˈtʃiːv/	*v.* 达到；完成	
achievement /əˈtʃiːvmənt/	*n.* 成就；成绩	
aim /eɪm/	*n.* 目标	
application /ˌæplɪˈkeɪʃn/	*n.* 申请；申请书；应用	
arithmetic /əˈrɪθmətɪk/	*n.* 算术	
attend /əˈtend/	*v.* 出席；参加	
attention /əˈtenʃn/	*n.* 注意	
bestseller /ˌbestˈselə(r)/	*n.* 畅销品；畅销书	
break /breɪk/	*v./n.* 间歇；休息	
break time	*n.* 课间休息	
candidate /ˈkændɪdeɪt/	*n.* 候选人；申请人	
certificate /səˈtɪfɪkət/	*n.* 证明；证明书	

challenge /ˈtʃælɪndʒ/	n./v.	挑战
challenging /ˈtʃælɪndʒɪŋ/	adj.	挑战性的；考验能力的
champion /ˈtʃæmpiən/	n.	冠军
championship /ˈtʃæmpiənʃɪp/	n.	锦标赛；冠军地位
college /ˈkɒlɪdʒ/	n.	学院
chapter /ˈtʃæptə(r)/	n.	章；篇；回
correction /kəˈrekʃn/	n.	改正；纠正
composition /ˌkɒmpəˈzɪʃn/	n.	作文；作品；作曲
curriculum /kəˈrɪkjələm/	n.	全部课程
degree /dɪˈɡriː/	n.	学位；度数
drama /ˈdrɑːmə/	n.	戏；剧
economics /ˌiːkəˈnɒmɪks/	n.	经济学
elementary /ˌelɪˈmentri/	adj.	初级的；基础的
essay /ˈeseɪ/	n.	文章
examiner /ɪɡˈzæmɪnə(r)/	n.	主考官；审查人
diploma /dɪˈpləʊmə/	n.	毕业文凭；文凭课程
fiction /ˈfɪkʃn/	n.	小说
non-fiction /ˌnɒn ˈfɪkʃn/	n.	非虚构作品
handwriting /ˈhændraɪtɪŋ/	n.	手写；书写
instructor /ɪnˈstrʌktə(r)/	n.	教练；导师
intermediate /ˌɪntəˈmiːdiət/	adj.	中级的；中等的；中间的
laboratory /ləˈbɒrətri/	n.	实验室
literature /ˈlɪtrətʃə(r)/	n.	文学；文学作品；文献
noticeboard /ˈnəʊtɪsbɔːd/	n.	告示牌
photography /fəˈtɒɡrəfi/	n.	摄影
primary school	n.	小学
present /ˈpreznt/	adj.	现在的；出席的
presentation /ˌpreznˈteɪʃn/	n.	幻灯片演示

presenter /prɪˈzentə(r)/	n.	演讲人；发言人
qualification /ˌkwɒlɪfɪˈkeɪʃn/	n.	资格
register /ˈredʒɪstə(r)/	v.	登记；注册
	n.	登记表；注册簿
rubber /ˈrʌbə(r)/	n.	橡皮；橡胶
secondary /ˈsekəndri/	adj.	次要的
technology /tekˈnɒlədʒi/	n.	技术

✔ 进阶加油站

◆ 高频短语

break up	（使）分裂；破碎；分手	break down	出故障；损坏
break out	（战争、矛盾或疾病）爆发	break one's word	食言；说话不算数
break the record	打破纪录	break the law/rule	违反法律／规定
break through	有新的重大发现；突破		

◆ 学科名称大总结

English	英语	geography	地理
Chinese	语文	music	音乐
literature	文学	chemistry	化学
maths/mathematics	数学	history	历史
biology	生物	P.E.	体育
physics	物理	art	艺术

EXERCISE

✓ MATCH

( ) 1. information	a. at a high or difficult level
( ) 2. university	b. a short informal letter
( ) 3. degree	c. action rather than ideas
( ) 4. certificate	d. a person who trains a person or team in sport
( ) 5. secondary	e. a series of lessons or lectures on a particular subject
( ) 6. laboratory	f. facts or details about sb./sth.
( ) 7. elementary	g. an examination of sb.'s knowledge or ability, consisting of questions for them to answer or activities for them to perform
( ) 8. coach	h. detailed information on how to do or use sth.
( ) 9. note	i. a particular standard or quality
( ) 10. advanced	j. an institution at the highest level of education where you can study for a degree or do research
( ) 11. instruction	k. not in a place because of illness, etc.
( ) 12. composition	l. an official document that may be used to prove that the facts it states are true
( ) 13. register	m. a piece of music or art, or a poem
( ) 14. handwriting	n. the amount or level of sth.
( ) 15. pupil	o. to record your/sb.'s/sth.'s name on an official list
( ) 16. test	p. in or connected with the first stages of a course of study
( ) 17. course	q. less important than sth. else
( ) 18. practice	r. writing that is done with a pen or pencil, not printed or typed
( ) 19. level	s. a person who is being taught, especially a child in a school
( ) 20. absent	t. a room or building used for scientific research, experiments, testing, etc.

☑ *MULTIPLE CHOICES*

(　　) 1. It is Jim's *practice* to read several books each Sunday.

　　　　A. exercise　　　　　　B. habit　　　　　　　C. convention

(　　) 2. Jane has finally *achieved* success.

　　　　A. carried　　　　　　B. managed　　　　　　C. attained

(　　) 3. The economic conference last week was *attended* by all of our shareholders.

　　　　A. presented　　　　　B. invited　　　　　　C. gone

(　　) 4. I've read all the available *literature* on gardening.

　　　　A. pieces of writing　B. letters　　　　　　C. notes

(　　) 5. James has finally become the world's new basketball *champion*.

　　　　A. fighter　　　　　　B. carrier　　　　　　C. title-holder

(　　) 6. The professor made a few small *corrections* to Lily's report.

　　　　A. revisions　　　　　B. reforms　　　　　　C. punishment

(　　) 7. Myths and legends have always been popular themes in *fiction*.

　　　　A. traditional short stories that teaches a moral lesson, especially one with

　　　　　　animals as characters

　　　　B. stories about imaginary people and events, not real ones

　　　　C. plays for the theatre, television or radio

(　　) 8. The doctor recommends me to *write down* my starting weight on the morning

　　　　before starting a diet.

　　　　A. record　　　　　　B. get down　　　　　　C. read down

(　　) 9. That green book is for *elementary* students.

　　　　A. essential　　　　　B. advanced　　　　　　C. primary

(　　) 10. Her *application* to the court was refused last Monday.

　　　　A. formal request　　B. practical use　　　　C. determination

(　　) 11. A few comments from the public are sufficient for *present* purposes.

　　　　A. now　　　　　　　B. current　　　　　　　C. nowadays

(　　) 12. The naughty children left dirty *marks* all over the floor.

　　　　A. spots　　　　　　　B. cuts　　　　　　　　C. scratches

(　　) 13. Being an excellent teacher in a college is *challenging* and rewarding.

A. difficult in an interesting way that tests the ability

B. dangerous or likely to fail

C. done or obtained without a lot of effort or problems

(   ) 14. The secretary has a *diploma* in marketing.

      A. certificate   B. evidence   C. proof

(   ) 15. My father is a driving *instructor*.

      A. trainer   B. manager   C. assistant

☑ FILLING THE BLANKS

examiners;	qualification;	curriculum;	technologies;	non-fiction;
chapter;	championships;	bookshelf;	attention;	photography;
beginners;	intermediate;	achievement;	presentation;	candidate

1. Juliana has won a gold medal at the European _____.

2. Have you read the book's third _____ on the social system?

3. The papers will be sent to _____ in another school.

4. The school has designed a course suitable for both _____ and advanced students.

5. You can find a Spanish-English dictionary on the _____ in my bedroom.

6. Are there any _____ stops between your house and the company?

7. Besides singing, _____ is also one of Jane's hobbies.

8. Bob has finally met the basic educational requirements for _____.

9. It is a remarkable _____ for such a young player.

10. Their company is still waiting for cheaper _____ to be developed, so they can reduce the product costs.

11. The students paid _____ to the teacher's lecture.

12. Some teachers tried to build computers into the regular school _____.

13. The series includes both fiction and _____.

14. Each student is required to give a slide and video _____ for the next class.

15. Marry being interviewed on TV now is a _____ for the office of governor.

SPEAKING

1. Which subject is the most difficult for you?

2. Do you like P.E.?

3. Have you ever participated in any competitions?

CHECK

1. challenge _____	2. attention _____	3. arithmetic _____
4. 冠军 _____	5. 成就 _____	6. 缺席 _____
7. biology _____	8. certificate _____	9. qualification _____
10. 告示牌 _____	11. 技术 _____	12. 候选人 _____
13. literature _____	14. correction _____	15. fiction _____
16. 爆发 _____	17. 食言 _____	18. 打破纪录 _____
19. break up _____	20. break through _____	

Day ② *Sports* 体育运动

VOCABULARY

✅ 基础词汇

词 汇		词 义	默写
bat /bæt/	*n.*	球棒；球拍；球板	
bathing suit	*n.*	游泳衣	
beach /biːtʃ/	*n.*	海滩；沙滩	
bicycle /ˈbaɪsɪkl/	*n.*	自行车	
catch /kætʃ/	*v.*	接住；抓住	
climb /klaɪm/	*v.*	攀登；爬	
club /klʌb/	*n.*	俱乐部；社团	
cricket /ˈkrɪkɪt/	*n.*	板球（运动）	
cycle /ˈsaɪkl/	*n.*	自行车	
	v.	骑自行车	
cycling /ˈsaɪklɪŋ/	*n.*	骑自行车运动（或活动）	
game /ɡeɪm/	*n.*	游戏；运动；比赛项目	
goal /ɡəʊl/	*n.*	目标；球门	
gym /dʒɪm/	*n.*	健身房；体育馆	
(gymnasium /dʒɪmˈneɪziəm/)			
kick /kɪk/	*v.*	踢；踹	
kit /kɪt/	*n.*	全套衣服及装备	
sports kit	*n.*	运动用品	
member /ˈmembə(r)/	*n.*	成员	
membership /ˈmembəʃɪp/	*n.*	会员资格；会员人数；会员	

prize /praɪz/	*n.*	奖；奖品；奖励
racket /ˈrækɪt/	*n.*	球拍
rest /rest/	*v.*	休息；放松
ride /raɪd/	*v.*	骑；驾驶
riding /ˈraɪdɪŋ/	*n.*	骑马
skateboard /ˈskeɪtbɔːd/	*n.*	滑板
sport /spɔːt/	*n.*	体育运动
sports centre	*n.*	体育中心
stadium /ˈsteɪdiəm/	*n.*	体育场；运动场
surf /sɜːf/	*v.*	冲浪
surfboard /ˈsɜːfbɔːd/	*n.*	冲浪板
swimming /ˈswɪmɪŋ/	*n.*	游泳
swimming pool	*n.*	游泳池
swimsuit /ˈswɪmsuːt/	*n.*	游泳衣
team /tiːm/	*n.*	队；组
throw /θrəʊ/	*v.*	投；掷；抛；扔
ticket /ˈtɪkɪt/	*n.*	票；券
tired /ˈtaɪəd/	*adj.*	疲倦的

✅ 重点词汇

词汇		词义	默写
athlete /ˈæθliːt/	*n.*	运动员	
athletics /æθˈletɪks/	*n.*	体育运动	
changing room	*n.*	更衣室	
compete /kəmˈpiːt/	*v.*	竞争	
competitor /kəmˈpetɪtə(r)/	*n.*	竞争对手	
competition /ˌkɒmpəˈtɪʃn/	*n.*	竞争	

contest /ˈkɒntest/	n.	比赛；竞赛
contestant /kənˈtestənt/	n.	比赛者；竞争者
court /kɔːt/	n.	球场；法院
tennis court	n.	网球场
cyclist /ˈsaɪklɪst/	n.	骑自行车的人
extreme sports	n.	极限运动
facility /fəˈsɪləti/	n.	设施；设备
fitness /ˈfɪtnəs/	n.	健壮；健康
goalkeeper /ˈɡəʊlkiːpə(r)/	n.	守门员
helmet /ˈhelmɪt/	n.	头盔
injure /ˈɪndʒə(r)/	v.	伤害；使受伤
injury /ˈɪndʒəri/	n.	伤害；损伤
jog /dʒɒɡ/	v.	慢跑
league /liːɡ/	n.	联合会；联赛；联盟
locker room	n.	更衣室
long jump	n.	跳远
motor racing	n.	赛道汽车赛
pitch /pɪtʃ/	n.	场地；球场
football pitch	n.	足球场
reserve /rɪˈzɜːv/	n.	替补队员
score /skɔː(r)/	n.	分数；得分
	v.	得分
season /ˈsiːzn/	n.	赛季；季节
shoot /ʃuːt/	v.	射击；射伤；射杀
shoot at the goal		射门
squash /skwɒʃ/	n.	壁球
	v.	把……压（或挤）变形
workout /ˈwɜːkaʊt/	n.	锻炼
yoga /ˈjəʊɡə/	n.	瑜伽

☑ 进阶加油站

◆ 构词法小知识

名词后缀	示例
-er/-or （表示从事某种职业的人）	act → actor　　dance → dancer sing → singer　　write → writer compete → competitor translate → translator
-ist （表示某种主义者或信仰者；表示从事某种职业、某种研究的人）	art → artist　　geology → geologist journal → journalist　　science → scientist social → socialist
-ician （表示在某方面擅长或从事某种职业的人）	music → musician　　history → historian

◆ 体育运动大总结

badminton	羽毛球运动	skiing	滑雪运动
basketball	篮球运动	skipping rope	跳绳
boating	划船（运动或消遣）	soccer	（英式）足球运动
baseball	棒球运动	surfing	冲浪运动
boxing	拳击运动	surfboarding	冲浪运动
football	足球运动	tennis	网球运动
golf	高尔夫球运动	table tennis	乒乓球运动
hockey	曲棍球运动	volleyball	排球运动
ice hockey	冰球运动	weightlifting	举重
sailing	帆船运动	wrestling	摔跤运动
skateboarding	滑板运动		

EXERCISE

MATCH

( ) 1. bat

( ) 2. goal

( ) 3. climb

( ) 4. rest

( ) 5. team

( ) 6. gym

( ) 7. ride

( ) 8. bicycle

( ) 9. kick

( ) 10. swimsuit

( ) 11. catch

( ) 12. skateboard

( ) 13. ticket

( ) 14. stadium

( ) 15. cycling

( ) 16. game

( ) 17. beach

( ) 18. throw

a. a room or hall with equipment for doing physical exercise

b. an area of sand or small stones, beside the sea or a lake

c. to stop and hold a moving object, especially in your hands

d. a group of people who work together at a particular job

e. a large sports ground surrounded by rows of seats and usually other buildings

f. a printed piece of paper that gives you the right to travel on a particular bus, train, etc. or to go into a theatre, etc.

g. to send sth. from your hand through the air by moving your hand or arm quickly

h. a piece of wood with a handle, made in various shapes and sizes, and used for hitting the ball in games

i. to hit sb./sth. with your foot

j. the sport or activity of riding a bicycle

k. to relax, sleep or do nothing after a period of activity or illness

l. a road vehicle with two wheels that you ride by pushing the pedals with your feet

m. something that you hope to achieve

n. to sit on and control a bicycle, motorcycle, etc.

o. an activity or a sport with rules in which people or teams compete against each other

p. to go up sth. towards the top

q. a short narrow board with small wheels at each end, which you stand on and ride as a sport

r. a piece of clothing worn for swimming

☑ *MULTIPLE CHOICES*

(   ) 1. Last weekend, a large number of bombs exploded, seriously *injuring* at least ten natives（本地人）.

      A. ruining   B. damaging   C. hurting

(   ) 2. James has won last year's title with a *score* of 99.8.

      A. mark   B. progress   C. achievement

(   ) 3. Susan is used to do a 30-minute *workout* every morning.

      A. work   B. housework   C. physical exercise

(   ) 4. I have never seen such thrilling *contests* before.

      A. tests   B. debates   C. competitions

(   ) 5. Nancy gets up early to *jog* round the park every morning.

      A. run slowly

      B. run quickly

      C. walk slowly

(   ) 6. He has been advised to *rest* for at least three weeks.

      A. break   B. relax   C. sleep

(   ) 7. He managed to *grasp* the key as it fell.

      A. catch   B. fetch   C. haul

(   ) 8. Sr. Black used to be a *member* of the Royal College of Surgeons.

      A. colleague   B. leader   C. fellow

(   ) 9. He has won the first *prize* in the singing contest.

      A. award   B. price   C. reward

(   ) 10. More than 1,000 *competitors* entered the race.

      A. objectors   B. colleagues   C. contestants

(   ) 11. Success is just a matter of setting *goals* and following them.

      A. achievements   B. targets   C. scores

(   ) 12. We passed long, hot afternoons *tossing* stones into the lake.

      A. throwing   B. thrusting   C. stroking

(   ) 13. Is there any entertaining *facility* now available?

      A. equipment   B. furniture   C. establishment

(   ) 14. Aron was so angry that he *kicked* the door hard.

      A. hit   B. moved   C. knocked

(   ) 15. Mary was looking *worn out*, but I didn't know what happened.

      A. down   B. tired   C. disappointed

✓ FILLING THE BLANKS

baseball;	athlete;	yoga;	compete;	extreme sports;
league;	jogging;	fitness;	helmet;	season;
shoot;	pitch;	cyclists;	goalkeeper;	locker room

1. The Lakers was the _____ champion last season.

2. I go _____ in the park every evening because it can improve my health.

3. You must wear the _____ to protect your head if you go there by motorcycle.

4. Peter was the football league's best _____.

5. Sheep _____ with cattle for sparse supplies of water.

6. If you want to learn something about bodybuilding, I would recommend this magazine about health and _____ to you.

7. _____ is a type of exercise in which you move your body into various positions to improve your breathing, and to relax your mind.

8. Mark Brown, the men's marathon world record holder, is a great _____.

9. A man was _____ in the leg in the gunfight.

10. He was the fastest man I ever saw on a football _____.

11. Every summer holiday, Jack and his friends play _____ on the ground behind the school.

12. Anna enjoys all kinds of _____, for example skydiving and bungee jumping.

13. On your way home, please look out for _____ and pedestrians.

14. In the _____, Vivian changed quickly.

15. Nicolas scored his first goal of the _____ on Monday.

LISTENING

Questions 1-6

For each question, write the correct answer in the gap. Write one or two words or a number or a date or a time.

You will hear a man talking to some cyclists about a cycling race.

Cycling race

The cycling race will start in front of the 1 _____ Hotel.

Cyclists need to arrive at the hotel before 2 _____.

The length of the race will be 3 _____.

The route is beside the 4 _____.

After the race, 5 _____ will have buffet for lunch.

Cyclists need to take 6 _____ and gloves.

扫码听录音

CHECK

1. beach _____

2. bat _____

3. stadium _____

4. 俱乐部 _____

5. 冲浪板 _____

6. 奖 _____

7. contest _____

8. court _____

9. injure _____

10. 运动员 _____

11. 竞争 _____

12. 头盔 _____

13. facility _____

14. jog _____

15. extreme sports ____

16. 游泳衣 _____

17. 守门员 _____

18. 瑜伽 _____

19. shoot _____

20. workout _____

Day ③ Communications and Technology
通信与科技

VOCABULARY

✅ 基础词汇

词汇	词义		默写
battery /ˈbætri/	n.	电池	
by post		邮寄	
CD player	n.	CD 播放机	
cell phone	n.	手机	
chat /tʃæt/	v.	闲聊；聊天	
chat room	n.	聊天室	
click /klɪk/	v.	点击	
computer /kəmˈpjuːtə(r)/	n.	计算机	
digital /ˈdɪdʒɪtl/	adj.	数码的	
digital camera	n.	数码相机	
dot /dɒt/	n.	点；小点	
download /ˌdaʊnˈləʊd/	v.	下载	
DVD player	n.	DVD 播放机	
electronic /ɪˌlekˈtrɒnɪk/	adj.	电子的	
envelope /ˈenvələʊp/	n.	信封	
file /faɪl/	n.	文件夹；文件	
Internet /ˈɪntənet/	n.	互联网	
keyboard /ˈkiːbɔːd/	n.	键盘	

latest /ˈleɪtɪst/	*adj.*	最新的；最近的
mouse /maʊs/	*n.*	鼠标
MP3 player	*n.*	MP3 播放器
net /net/	*n.*	网
online /ˌɒnˈlaɪn/	*adj.*	在线的
password /ˈpɑːswɜːd/	*n.*	密码
post /pəʊst/	*n.*	邮政；邮递；邮寄
printer /ˈprɪntə(r)/	*n.*	打印机
screen /skriːn/	*n.*	屏幕
software /ˈsɒftweə(r)/	*n.*	软件
telephone /ˈtelɪfəʊn/	*n.*	电话
web /web/	*n.*	网状物
web page	*n.*	网页
website /ˈwebsaɪt/	*n.*	网站

✓ 重点词汇

词汇	词义		默写
access /ˈækses/	*v.*	访问，存取（计算机文件）	
answerphone /ˈɑːnsəfəʊn/	*n.*	电话答录机	
application /ˌæplɪˈkeɪʃn/	*n.*	应用程序	
calculator /ˈkælkjuleɪtə(r)/	*n.*	计算器	
connect /kəˈnekt/	*v.*	连接	
connection /kəˈnekʃn/	*n.*	连接；旅行交通工具	
data /ˈdeɪtə/	*n.*	数据；资料；材料	
delete /dɪˈliːt/	*v.*	删除	
dial /ˈdaɪəl/	*v.*	拨（电话号码）	
disc /dɪsk/	*n.*	（计算机）光碟，光盘	
drag /dræg/	*v.*	拖；拽；拉	

engaged /ɪnˈɡeɪdʒd/	adj.	忙于；被占用的
equipment /ɪˈkwɪpmənt/	n.	设备
fax /fæks/	n.	传真机；传真信件；传真电文
hang up		挂断电话
hardware /ˈhɑːdweə(r)/	n.	硬件
home page	n.	（网站）主页，首页
headphones /ˈhedfəʊnz/	n.	耳机
install /ɪnˈstɔːl/	v.	安装
invent /ɪnˈvent/	v.	发明；创造
mouse mat	n.	鼠标垫
operator /ˈɒpəreɪtə(r)/	n.	技工；操作人员
out of date		过时的
parcel /ˈpɑːsl/	n.	包裹
pause /pɔːz/	n./v.	暂停；停顿
podcast /ˈpɒdkɑːst/	n.	播客
postcard /ˈpəʊstkɑːd/	n.	明信片
print /prɪnt/	n./v.	打印
remote control	n.	遥控
robot /ˈrəʊbɒt/	n.	机器人
selfie /ˈselfiː/	n.	自拍照
take a selfie		自拍
server /ˈsɜːvə(r)/	n.	服务器
sign up		签订；报名（参加课程）
smartphone /ˈsmɑːtfəʊn/	n.	智能手机
soundtrack /ˈsaʊndtræk/	n.	（电影）声带；电影原声音乐（或配音、对白）
switch on		开启；打开
switch off		关掉；关上
video clip	n.	视频；视频剪辑
volume /ˈvɒljuːm/	n.	量；额；音量；体积
webcam /ˈwebkæm/	n.	网络摄像机；网络摄影机

✅ 进阶加油站

◆ 构词法小知识

CD (compact disc)	光盘
DJ (disc jockey)	唱片节目主持人
IT (information technology)	信息技术
PC (personal computer)	个人电脑
DVD (digital videodisc）	数字影碟

EXERCISE

✅ MATCH

(　) 1. hardware

(　) 2. keyboard

(　) 3. chat

(　) 4. operator

(　) 5. website

(　) 6. data

(　) 7. fax

(　) 8. drag

(　) 9. pause

(　) 10. postcard

(　) 11. dot

(　) 12. calculator

(　) 13. download

(　) 14. mouse

a. a machine that sends and receives documents in an electronic form along telephone wires and then prints them

b. to pull sb./sth. along with effort and difficulty

c. a period of time during which sb. stops talking or stops what they are doing

d. a small electronic device for calculating with numbers

e. to get data from another computer, usually using the Internet

f. a small round mark, especially one that is printed

g. the set of keys for operating a computer or typewriter

h. a card used for sending messages by post without an envelope

i. a person who operates equipment or a machine

j. a place connected to the Internet, where a company or an organization, or an individual person, puts information

k. the machinery and electronic parts of a computer system

l. facts or information, especially when examined and used to find out things or to make decisions

m. to talk in a friendly informal way to sb.

n. a small device that is moved by hand across a surface to control the movement of the cursor on a computer screen

☑ *MULTIPLE CHOICES*

( ) 1. All of these rooms are *installed* with smoke alarms.

    A. fitted   B. stalled   C. decorated

( ) 2. It is commonly agreed that students must *have access to* good resources.

    A. make use of   B. be applicable to   C. have the opportunity to use

( ) 3. They sent *parcels* of food and clothing to soldiers in the front line.

    A. luggage   B. packages   C. baggage

( ) 4. The two towns are *connected* by bus services.

    A. linked   B. contacted   C. related

( ) 5. Mikel is now *engaged on* his first novel.

    A. attracted by   B. filled with   C. busy finishing

( ) 6. Do you know who *invented* the steam engine?

    A. devised   B. discovered   C. destroyed

( ) 7. In tomorrow's meeting, the leaders will discuss how the *volume* of sales might

    be reduced.

    A. number   B. amount   C. cubage

( ) 8. After resignation, Jane *deleted* all the files from the computer system.

    A. stored   B. removed   C. reserved

( ) 9. I got the opportunity to drive the *latest* model.

    A. very new   B. nearest   C. oldest

( ) 10. His job is to write *software* for a big computer company.

    A. hardware   B. computer programs   C. wares

( ) 11. I'll send the original files to you *by post*.

    A. by sending e-mails   B. by writing letters   C. by mail

( ) 12. These laws were *out of date* and confusing.

    A. fashionable   B. modern   C. outdated

(   ) 13. You can *sign up for* the painting course through the network.

       A. register   B. cancel   C. complete

(   ) 14. You must give the *password* if you want to go inside.

       A. passport   B. secret word   C. pass through

☑ FILLING THE BLANKS

connections;	hung up;	digital;	electronic;	Internet;
web page;	files;	print;	hardware;	application;
switched off;	webcam;	dialed;	fax;	soundtrack

1. You can buy goods over the _____ and distance is no problem with modern telecommunications.

2. After a one-week study of computer design, we learned how to create a new _____.

3. Jacob _____ the coffee-machine before he left the company.

4. Every day, a stack of _____ awaits Lily on her desk.

5. My mom _____ the phone before I said a word.

6. I would recommend this video-clip _____ to you.

7. Beijing has excellent air and rail _____ to the rest places of China.

8. With a _____, you can take pictures that can be viewed on a website.

9. The journal is available in paper and _____ form.

10. You need a piece of _____ that costs about $500 to protect your computer.

11. I'm asking Lucy to _____ a copy of the document for you.

12. This is exactly the _____ to a movie called *Judgement Night*.

13. He couldn't help lifting the phone and _____ Anna's number.

14. They have developed a new kind of _____ cameras which attract lots of young people.

15. My aunt sent me a long _____, saying she didn't need any help.

 READING

Questions 1-6

For each question, choose the correct answer.

Robots

A true robot is a machine that can move about and do different jobs without human help. The word 'robot' was 1 _____ used to describe factory workers, and that is just what the majority of actual robots are. However, robots work without 2 _____ a rest. This makes them good at doing 3 _____ or dangerous jobs. Although they have not yet replaced human workers, robots have made factories 4 _____ more efficient.

Children are often keen 5 _____ robot toys. One robot dog called Aibo can sleep and play. It first went on sale in 1999 in Japan. 6 _____ then it has become cheaper to buy and more reliable. The latest models can do a large number of different things. They can even recognise their owner's face.

1. A. eventually	B. actually	C. originally	D. really
2. A. asking	B. having	C. doing	D. making
3. A. boring	B. exciting	C. relaxing	D. innovative
4. A. many	B. any	C. all	D. much
5. A. in	B. on	C. about	D. at
6. A. Since	B. From	C. Although	D. Because

CHECK

1. battery _____

2. digital camera _____

3. download _____

4. 闲聊；聊天 _____

5. 信封 _____

6. 软件 _____

7. calculator _____

8. delete _____

9. dial _____

10. 硬件 _____

11. （网站）主页，首页 _____

12. 安装 _____

13. selfie _____

14. postcard _____

15. smartphone _____

Day ④ *Entertainment* 娱乐

VOCABULARY

✅ 基础词汇

词汇	词义	默写
actor /ˈæktə(r)/	*n.* 演员	
adventure /ədˈventʃə(r)/	*n.* 冒险	
art /ɑːt/	*n.* 艺术	
board game	*n.* 棋类游戏	
book /bʊk/	*v.* 预订 *n.* 书	
camera /ˈkæmərə/	*n.* 照相机	
camp /kæmp/	*n.* 营地；度假营	
camping /ˈkæmpɪŋ/	*n.* 野营度假	
campsite /ˈkæmpsaɪt/	*n.* 野营地；度假营地	
card /kɑːd/	*n.* 卡片	
cartoon /kɑːˈtuːn/	*n.* 卡通片；动画片	
chess /tʃes/	*n.* 国际象棋	
cinema /ˈsɪnəmə/	*n.* 电影院	
concert /ˈkɒnsət/	*n.* 音乐会	
dancer /ˈdɑːnsə(r)/	*n.* 跳舞者	
draw /drɔː/	*v.* 画	
drawing /ˈdrɔːɪŋ/	*n.* 图画；绘画（艺术）	
disco /ˈdɪskəʊ/	*n.* 迪斯科舞厅（或舞会）	
festival /ˈfestɪvl/	*n.* 节日	
fun /fʌn/	*n.* 乐趣	
go out	出门参加社交活动	

guitar /gɪˈtɑː(r)/	*n.*	吉他	
hip hop	*n.*	嘻哈音乐	
instrument /ˈɪnstrəmənt/	*n.*	乐器；器械；仪器	
laugh /lɑːf/	*v.*	笑	
listen to		听	
look at		看	
museum /mjuˈziːəm/	*n.*	博物馆	
music /ˈmjuːzɪk/	*n.*	音乐	
musician /mjuˈzɪʃn/	*n.*	音乐家	
opera /ˈɒprə/	*n.*	歌剧	
painter /ˈpeɪntə(r)/	*n.*	画家	
programme /ˈprəʊɡræm/	*n.*	程序；节目	
puzzle /ˈpʌzl/	*n.*	智力游戏；谜	
	v.	迷惑；使困惑	
sightseeing /ˈsaɪtsiːɪŋ/	*n.*	观光；游览	

☑ 重点词汇

词 汇	词 义		默 写
audience /ˈɔːdiəns/	*n.*	观众；听众；读者	
ballet /ˈbæleɪ/	*n.*	芭蕾舞	
cheers /tʃɪəz/	*exclam.*	干杯	
cheerful /ˈtʃɪəfl/	*adj.*	快乐的；高兴的；令人愉快的	
circus /ˈsɜːkəs/	*n.*	马戏团	
classical music	*n.*	古典音乐	
comedy /ˈkɒmədi/	*n.*	喜剧；喜剧片	
comic /ˈkɒmɪk/	*adj.*	滑稽的；使人发笑的	

display /dɪˈspleɪ/	v.	陈列；展出；展示
disc jockey(DJ)	n.	唱片节目主持人
enjoyable /ɪnˈdʒɔɪəbl/	adj.	有乐趣的；令人愉快的
entertain /ˌentəˈteɪn/	v.	娱乐；使快乐
entertainment /ˌentəˈteɪnmənt/	n.	娱乐活动
film-maker /ˈfɪlm meɪkə(r)/	n.	电影制作人
film star	n.	电影明星
firework /ˈfaɪəwɜːk/	n.	烟火；烟花
folk music	n.	民间音乐
hang out		常去某处；泡在某处
hero /ˈhɪərəʊ/	n.	英雄；男主角
heroine /ˈherəʊɪn/	n.	女英雄；女主角
hit song	n.	流行歌曲
horror /ˈhɒrə(r)/	n.	恐惧；震惊
jazz music	n.	爵士乐
keen /kiːn/	adj.	热切的
leisure /ˈleʒə(r)/	n.	闲暇
magic /ˈmædʒɪk/	n.	魔法；魔术
orchestra /ˈɔːkɪstrə/	n.	管弦乐队
perform /pəˈfɔːm/	v.	演出；表演
performance /pəˈfɔːməns/	n.	演出；表演
performer /pəˈfɔːmə(r)/	n.	表演者
poem /ˈpəʊɪm/	n.	诗
presenter /prɪˈzentə(r)/	n.	节目主持人
production /prəˈdʌkʃn/	n.	生产
refreshment /rɪˈfreʃmənt/	n.	恢复活力；食物和饮料

relax /rɪˈlæks/	*v.*	放松；（使）冷静，放心
relaxed /rɪˈlækst/	*adj.*	放松的
rock music	*n.*	摇滚乐
romance /rəʊˈmæns/	*n.*	浪漫氛围；传奇色彩
romantic /rəʊˈmæntɪk/	*adj.*	浪漫的
scene /siːn/	*n.*	场面；情景；景色；风光
series /ˈsɪəriːz/	*n.*	一系列
soap opera	*n.*	肥皂剧
stage /steɪdʒ/	*n.*	舞台
thriller /ˈθrɪlə(r)/	*n.*	惊险小说（或戏剧、电影）

✅ 进阶加油站

◆ 高频短语

● **be keen on sth.** 热衷于某事；对某事着迷，有兴趣

eg. *I am not keen on physics.* 我不喜欢物理。

● **be keen to do sth.** 渴望做某事；喜欢做某事

eg. *The children are keen to visit the castle.* 孩子们渴望去参观城堡。

● **be keen on doing sth.** 渴望做某事；喜欢做某事

eg. *My father is keen on collecting coins.* 我的爸爸喜欢收集硬币。

◆ 英式英语 & 美式英语

中文	英式英语	美式英语
电影	film	movie
电影明星	film star	movie star
电影院	cinema	movie theater/ theater

EXERCISE

✓ MATCH

( ) 1. actor

( ) 2. cheers

( ) 3. campsite

( ) 4. comic

( ) 5. perform

( ) 6. musician

( ) 7. drawing

( ) 8. sightseeing

( ) 9. folk music

( ) 10. thriller

( ) 11. painter

( ) 12. draw

( ) 13. heroine

( ) 14. orchestra

( ) 15. refreshment

( ) 16. disc jockey

a. the activity of visiting interesting buildings and places as a tourist

b. an artist who paints pictures

c. a large group of people who play various musical instruments together, led by a conductor

d. music in the traditional style of a country or community

e. a book, play or film with an exciting story, especially one about crime or spying

f. to entertain an audience by playing a piece of music, acting in a play, etc.

g. a person whose job is to introduce and play recorded popular music, on radio or television or at a club

h. a word that people say to each other as they lift up their glasses to drink

i. to make pictures, or a picture of sth., with a pencil, pen or chalk

j. amusing and making you laugh

k. a place where people on holiday can put up their tents, park their camper, etc.

l. a picture made using a pencil or pen rather than paint

m. a person who plays a musical instrument or writes music, especially as a job

n. a person who performs on the stage, on television or in films, especially as a profession

o. food and drink

p. a girl or woman who is admired by many for doing sth. brave or good

☑ *MULTIPLE CHOICES*

(   ) 1. Judy wasn't *enthusiastic about* sports.

   A. accustomed to   B. good at   C. keen on

(   ) 2. Lily was always *cheerful*.

   A. happy   B. cheers   C. stirring

(   ) 3. Children's television not only *entertains* but also teaches.

   A. amuses   B. encourages   C. accepts

(   ) 4. Last Tuesday, Anna *displayed* her wound to the nine gentlemen of the jury, and all

   of them were deeply impressed.

   A. played   B. saw   C. showed

(   ) 5. Everything's OK. You should *relax* and stop worrying about it.

   A. become more nervous   B. become calmer   C. tense your muscles

(   ) 6. I felt numb with *horror* when I noticed the man behind the door.

   A. humor   B. great shock   C. honour

(   ) 7. My husband always *puzzles* me and causes me anxiety.

   A. confuses   B. frightens   C. doesn't understand

(   ) 8. We were attracted by the beautiful *view* of the Neva River.

   A. event   B. scene   C. incident

(   ) 9. The car won't go into *production* before late 2025.

   A. manufacture   B. outcome   C. work

(   ) 10. I thought they were *laughing at* me because I was ugly.

   A. smiling at   B. making fun of   C. encouraging

(   ) 11. Her writings reached a wide *audience* after she died.

   A. readers   B. interviewers   C. watchers

(   ) 12. Playing computer games is a relaxing way to fill my *leisure* time.

   A. lazy   B. spare   C. available

(   ) 13. The authorities have a *series* of meetings with students this week.

   A. little   B. succession   C. set

(   ) 14. The National Day from October 1st is a seven-day *festival* for Chinese people.

       A. attempt   B. holiday   C. work

☑ FILLING THE BLANKS

museum;	enjoyable;	magic;	ballets;	stage;
presenter;	romantic;	instrument;	performance;	entertainment;
relaxed;	camping;	hero;	circus;	comedy

1. *Swan Lake* is one of the best-known _____.

2. My real ambition was to work in a _____ and bring happiness to people.

3. The movie that we are going to watch tomorrow is a romantic _____.

4. Playing poker in the evening is a typical family _____.

5. The film is much more _____ than I had expected, which is well worth-seeing.

6. He was a great national _____ who had inspired millions of people.

7. They have given a wonderful _____ of *Carmen*.

8. Julia used to work as a _____ of a live radio programme.

9. As soon as I had finished all the tasks, I felt a lot more _____.

10. The actor was applauded as he came on _____.

11. Vivian and Aron are making plans to go _____ in the wild next weekend.

12. Learning a musical _____ can arouse a child's interest in music.

13. My father has prepared a _____ candlelit dinner for my mother to give her a surprise.

14. They believe in science instead of _____.

15. Three years ago, he donated all his art collection to the New York Metropolitan _____ of Art.

✅ *WRITING*

Write your answer in about **100 words**.
You see this announcement on an English-language website.

Articles wanted!

Young people live in a world which is increasingly connected.

Do you like chatting online?

How important is social media to you?

Write an article answering these questions, and we'll publish the best ones on our website.

CHECK

1. adventure _____

2. festival _____

3. cartoon _____

4. 野营度假 _____

5. 国际象棋 _____

6. 音乐会 _____

7. museum _____

8. musician _____

9. programme _____

10. 观众 _____

11. 喜剧 _____

12. 烟火 _____

13. romance _____

14. stage _____

15. thriller _____

16. 吉他 _____

17. 观光 _____

18. 芭蕾舞 _____

19. poem _____

20. heroine _____

Day ⑤ *Media* 媒体

VOCABULARY

✅ 基础词汇

词　汇		词　义	默写
advertisement /ədˈvɜːtɪsmənt/	*n.*	广告	
article /ˈɑːtɪkl/	*n.*	（报刊上的）文章，报道	
blog /blɒg/	*n.*	博客	
CD player	*n.*	CD 播放机	
contact /ˈkɒntækt/	*n.*	联系；联络；接触	
conversation /ˌkɒnvəˈseɪʃn/	*n.*	交谈；谈话	
DVD player	*n.*	DVD 播放机	
exhibition /ˌeksɪˈbɪʃn/	*n.*	展览；展出	
group /gruːp/	*n.*	组；群；批；类	
magazine /ˌmægəˈziːn/	*n.*	杂志	
MP3 player	*n.*	MP3 播放器	
news /njuːz/	*n.*	新闻	
newspaper /ˈnjuːzpeɪpə(r)/	*n.*	报纸	
photograph /ˈfəʊtəgrɑːf/	*n.*	照片	
programme /ˈprəʊgræm/	*n.*	节目	
screen /skriːn/	*n.*	屏幕	
speaker /ˈspiːkə(r)/	*n.*	发言者；演讲者	
television /ˈtelɪvɪʒn/	*n.*	电视机；电视	

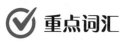 重点词汇

词 汇		词 义	默写
admission /ədˈmɪʃn/	n.	准许加入；加入权；进入权	
advanced /ədˈvɑːnst/	adj.	先进的	
advert /ˈædvɜːt/	n.	广告	
advertise /ˈædvətaɪz/	v.	登广告	
agency /ˈeɪdʒənsi/	n.	服务机构；代理机构	
announce /əˈnaʊns/	v.	宣布；宣告	
announcement /əˈnaʊnsmənt/	n.	公告；通告	
bestseller /ˌbestˈselə(r)/	n.	畅销书	
blogger /ˈblɒgə(r)/	n.	博客作者	
celebrity /səˈlebrəti/	n.	名人	
channel /ˈtʃænl/	n.	频道	
documentary /ˌdɒkjuˈmentri/	n.	纪录片	
headline /ˈhedlaɪn/	n.	（报纸的）大字标题	
headphones /ˈhedfəʊnz/	n.	耳机	
interval /ˈɪntəvl/	n.	间隔	
interviewer /ˈɪntəvjuːə(r)/	n.	采访者	
interviewee /ˌɪntəvjuːˈiː/	n.	参加面试者；受访者	
journalist /ˈdʒɜːnəlɪst/	n.	新闻记者	
recording /rɪˈkɔːdɪŋ/	n.	录音；视频；录像	
report /rɪˈpɔːt/	n.	报告；报道；调查报告	
reporter /rɪˈpɔːtə(r)/	n.	记者	
review /rɪˈvjuː/	v.	评论；回顾；复习	
social media	n.	网络社交媒体	
studio /ˈstjuːdiəʊ/	n.	演播室；录音室；录音棚	
talk show	n.	访谈节目	
update /ˌʌpˈdeɪt/	v.	更新	
user /ˈjuːzə(r)/	n.	用户	

✅ 进阶加油站

◆ 社交媒体词汇

Facebook	脸书	Twitter	推特
Wechat	微信	Subscription	订阅
Moments	朋友圈	follow	（在社交网站上）关注
Microblog	微博	unfollow	（在社交网站上）取消关注
Sina Microblog	新浪微博	follower	关注者 / 粉丝
trending topic	热门话题	QR code	二维码
sticker	表情	comment	评论
send a sticker	发表情	hit the like button	点赞

◆ 构词法小知识

TV (television)	电视
APP (application)	应用软件
VOA (Voice of America)	美国之声（广播电台）
WTO (World Trade Organization)	世界贸易组织
BBC (British Broadcasting Corporation)	英国广播公司
IOC (International Olympic Committee)	国际奥委会

EXERCISE

✅ MATCH

( ) 1. magazine

( ) 2. newspaper

( ) 3. advertise

( ) 4. studio

( ) 5. update

( ) 6. contact

( ) 7. exhibition

( ) 8. group

( ) 9. interval

( ) 10. interviewee

( ) 11. documentary

( ) 12. agency

( ) 13. announce

( ) 14. celebrity

( ) 15. reporter

a. the act of communicating with sb., especially regularly

b. to tell people sth. officially, especially about a decision, plans, etc.

c. a film or a radio or television programme giving facts about sth.

d. a collection of things, for example works of art, that are shown to the public

e. to tell the public about a product or a service in order to encourage people to buy or to use it

f. a business or an organization that provides a particular service especially on behalf of other businesses or organizations

g. a person who collects and reports news for newspapers, radio or television

h. a set of large printed sheets of paper containing news, articles, advertisements, etc. and published every day or every week

i. the person who answers the questions in an interview

j. a number of people or things that are together in the same place or that are connected in some way

k. to add the most recent information to sth.

l. a famous person

m. a room where radio or television programmes are recorded and broadcast from, or where music is recorded

n. a type of large thin book with a paper cover that you can buy every week or month

o. a period of time between two events

✅ *MULTIPLE CHOICES*

(   ) 1. Bob applied for *admission* to the College of Foreign Languages in Tsinghua University.

     A. rejection   B. permission   C. license

(   ) 2. The country is a superpower equipped with the most *advanced* military technology in the world.

     A. developed   B. cultured   C. developing

(   ) 3. Holtan will *announce* tomorrow that he is resigning from office.

     A. forecast   B. indicate   C. tell people publicly

(   ) 4. That famous singer did not perform until after the *interval*.

     A. interview   B. short break   C. medium

(   ) 5. In 2020, at the age of 10, Helen suddenly became a *celebrity*.

     A. fame   B. celebration   C. famous person

(   ) 6. The scandal was in the *headline* for seven days until another scandal was revealed.

     A. newspaper title   B. head   C. top

(   ) 7. By mid-January, this novel was the *most popular book*.

     A. bestseller   B. hot topic   C. popularity

(   ) 8. The duty of a *journalist* is to collect and write news stories for newspapers, magazines, television, or radio.

     A. interviewer   B. interviewee   C. newspaperman

(   ) 9. The education committee will publish the *official document* on the educational reform for the next decade.

     A. report   B. interview   C. data

(   ) 10. My friends and I still keep in *contact* with each other after graduating for 15 years.

     A. connect   B. touch   C. link

(   ) 11. When we arrived at our hometown, Tom said he wanted to take some *photographs* of the local houses.

     A. pictures   B. paintings   C. cameras

(   ) 12. Among the *speakers* at the conference, the man wearing a pair of glasses was Brady.

     A. a person who gives a talk or makes a speech

B. a person who talks in a particular way or who talks a lot

C. a person who is able to describe their ideas and feelings clearly to others

(   ) 13. I had a telephone *conversation* with her yesterday.

     A. formal talk   B. informal talk   C. official meeting

(   ) 14. Sunny decided to make her *announcement* after talks with the president.

     A. declaration   B. prediction   C. underline

☑ FILLING THE BLANKS

interviewees;	review;	advertisement;	exhibition;	social media;
reporter;	users;	screen;	agency;	studio;
documentary;	interval;	headphones;	recording;	article

1. We have put an _____ in the local paper to sell our cars.

2. They usually hire servants through that reliable _____.

3. We watched a TV _____ on homelessness last night.

4. He usually cycles while listening to the local programme on _____.

5. There are so many _____ that stand out as memorable that the boss doesn't know how to choose.

6. Can you help me to find out a video _____ of a police interview last Monday?

7. You must _____ all the notes covering each course if you want to get an A.

8. _____ can change their password and personal setting.

9. I would like to invite you to go to an _____ of ancient art tomorrow.

10. Have you seen the _____ about a young fashion designer——Jack Jones on yesterday's newspaper?

11. Staring at the television _____ for such a long time will do harm to your eyes.

12. The signal is repeated after a short _____ of time.

13. She shares her life at the farm through photos, videos and written posts on _____ platforms.

14. Susan is recording her third album in the _____.

15. I hope I can be a _____ in the *New York Times* one day.

 **WRITING**

Write your answer in about 100 words .

You see this announcement on an English-language website.

Aticles wanted!

If you are interested in social media, we want to hear from you.

Should there be age restrictions for social media sites?

Do you think there is a concern of safety on social media sites?

The best articles answering these questions will be published next month.

Write your article.

 **CHECK**

1. conversation _____

2. magazine _____

3. programme _____

4. 广告 _____

5. 屏幕 _____

6. 演讲者 _____

7. exhibition _____

8. article _____

9. newspaper _____

10. 博客 _____

11. 博客作者 _____

12. 畅销书 _____

13. agency _____

14. reporter _____

15. interviewer _____

16. 回顾 _____

17. 名人 _____

18. 频道 _____

19. headline _____

20. update _____

Day ⑥ *Family and Friends* 家庭与朋友

VOCABULARY

✅ 基础词汇

词汇		词义	默写
aunt /ɑːnt/	*n.*	姑母；姨母；伯母；婶母	
brother /ˈbrʌðə(r)/	*n.*	哥哥；弟弟	
child /tʃaɪld/	*n.*	儿童；小孩	
cousin /ˈkʌzn/	*n.*	堂兄（或弟、姊、妹）；表兄（或弟、姊、妹）	
daddy /ˈdædi/	*n.*	爸爸	
daughter /ˈdɔːtə(r)/	*n.*	女儿	
family /ˈfæməli/	*n.*	家庭	
father /ˈfɑːðə(r)/	*n.*	父亲	
friend /frend/	*n.*	朋友	
friendly /ˈfrendli/	*adj.*	友好的；友爱的	
first name	*n.*	名字	
girl /ɡɜːl/	*n.*	女孩	
grandchild /ˈɡræntʃaɪld/	*n.*	（外）孙子，孙女	
granddaughter /ˈɡrændɔːtə(r)/	*n.*	（外）孙女	
grandfather /ˈɡrænfɑːðə(r)/	*n.*	（外）祖父	
grandma /ˈɡrænmɑː/	*n.*	（外）祖母；奶奶；外婆	
grandmother /ˈɡrænmʌðə(r)/	*n.*	（外）祖母	
grandpa /ˈɡrænpɑː/	*n.*	（外）祖父；爷爷；外公	
grandparent /ˈɡrænpeərənt/	*n.*	（外）祖父母	
grandson /ˈɡrænsʌn/	*n.*	孙子；外孙	

granny /ˈgræni/	n.	奶奶
grow up		长大
guest /gest/	n.	客人；宾客；旅客；房客
guy /gaɪ/	n.	小伙子；家伙
husband /ˈhʌzbənd/	n.	丈夫
kid /kɪd/	n.	小孩；年轻人
married /ˈmærid/	adj.	已婚的；婚姻的
mother /ˈmʌðə(r)/	n.	母亲
neighbour /ˈneɪbə(r)/	n.	邻居
parent /ˈpeərənt/	n.	父亲；母亲
penfriend /ˈpenfrend/	n.	笔友
sister /ˈsɪstə(r)/	n.	姐姐；妹妹
son /sʌn/	n.	儿子
surname /ˈsɜːneɪm/	n.	姓
teenager /ˈtiːneɪdʒə(r)/	n.	（13 至 19 岁之间的）青少年
uncle /ˈʌŋkl/	n.	叔父；姨父；伯父；姑父
wife /waɪf/	n.	妻子

✓ 重点词汇

词汇	词义		默写
anniversary /ˌænɪˈvɜːsəri/	n.	周年纪念日	
boyfriend /ˈbɔɪfrend/	n.	男朋友	
babysit /ˈbeɪbisɪt/	v.	当临时保姆	
babysitter /ˈbeɪbisɪtə(r)/	n.	临时保姆	
bride /braɪd/	n.	新娘	
bridegroom /ˈbraɪdɡruːm/	n.	新郎	
childhood /ˈtʃaɪldhʊd/	n.	童年	

female /ˈfiːmeɪl/	*adj.* 女性的 *n.* 女子
girlfriend /ˈɡɜːlfrend/	*n.* 女朋友
honey /ˈhʌni/	*n.* 蜂蜜；亲爱的
honeymoon /ˈhʌnimuːn/	*n.* 蜜月
housewife /ˈhaʊswaɪf/	*n.* 家庭主妇
male /meɪl/	*adj.* 男性的 *n.* 男性
marriage /ˈmærɪdʒ/	*n.* 结婚
marry /ˈmæri/	*v.* 结婚
middle-aged /ˌmɪdlˈeɪdʒd/	*adj.* 中年的
neighbourhood /ˈneɪbəhʊd/	*n.* 居民区；街区
niece /niːs/	*n.* 侄女；外甥女
nephew /ˈnefjuː/	*n.* 侄子；外甥
newborn /ˈnjuːbɔːn/	*adj.* 新生的；初生的
pregnant /ˈpreɡnənt/	*adj.* 怀孕的
private /ˈpraɪvət/	*adj.* 私有的；私人的；私立的
split up	分手；断绝关系
spoil /spɔɪl/	*v.* 破坏；溺爱
trust /trʌst/	*v./n.* 信任

✅ 进阶加油站

◆ "姓"与"名"

姓	名	全名
surname	—	—
last name	first name	full name
family name	given name	—

 **EXERCISE**

✅ MATCH

(   ) 1. cousin

(   ) 2. husband

(   ) 3. female

(   ) 4. anniversary

(   ) 5. childhood

(   ) 6. wife

(   ) 7. babysitter

(   ) 8. marriage

(   ) 9. niece

(   ) 10. grandchild

(   ) 11. neighbour

(   ) 12. bridegroom

(   ) 13. pregnant

(   ) 14. surname

(   ) 15. teenager

(   ) 16. private

(   ) 17. friendly

(   ) 18. guest

(   ) 19. friend

(   ) 20. kid

a. a person who lives next to you or near you

b. having a baby or young animal developing inside her/its body

c. a person who is between 13 and 19 years old

d. being a woman or a girl

e. a man on his wedding day

f. belonging to or for the use of a particular person or group; not for public use

g. a child of your aunt or uncle

h. a person that you have invited to your house or to a particular event that you are paying for

i. a person who takes care of babies or children while their parents are away from home and is usually paid to do this

j. a child or young person

k. a person you know well and like, and who is not usually a member of your family

l. the period of sb's life when they are a child

m. the daughter of your brother or sister

n. the man that a woman is married to

o. a name shared by all the members of a family

p. a date that is an exact number of years after the date of an important or special event

q. a child of your son or daughter

r. the legal relationship between a husband and wife

s. behaving in a kind and pleasant way because you like sb. or want to help them

t. the woman that a man is married to

☑ *MULTIPLE CHOICES*

(   ) 1. I was the only hotel *guest* last night.

      A. company   B. customer   C. host

(   ) 2. For the first five years of our *married* life, we lived in London.

      A. marital   B. divorced   C. separated

(   ) 3. It might be better if we discuss this *in private*.

      A. in public

      B. in front of people

      C. with nobody else present

(   ) 4. She's just *split up* with her boyfriend.

      A. broken down   B. torn up   C. broken up

(   ) 5. You should never let mistakes *spoil* your life.

      A. enrich   B. destroy   C. injure

(   ) 6. Think over what they have done! They've betrayed our *trust*.

      A. belief   B. doubt   C. suspicion

(   ) 7. After marrying for 2 years, Luna *got pregnant*.

      A. got a child

      B. had a baby developing in her body

      C. bore a child

(   ) 8. I am planning a 20th birthday party for my *nephew*.

      A. the daughter of my sister

      B. the son of my sister

      C. the child of my aunt

(   ) 9. There are only one *female* teacher in my high school.

      A. man   B. woman   C. male

(   ) 10. I just know her *first name* was Mary, and can you find her for me?

      A. surname   B. given name   C. family name

(   ) 11. She wrote to *her aunt* in Chongqing and invited her to the wedding ceremony in August.

      A. the wife of her uncle

B. the sister of her nephew

C. the sister of her niece

(　　) 12. 'Never be frightened by failure, *kid*,' a passerby comforts him.

    A. teenager　　　　　B. adult　　　　　C. child

(　　) 13. She *grew up* in a small village of Guangxi province.

    A. developed　　　　　B. grew tall　　　　　C. was brought up

(　　) 14. Vegas and Nancy decided to *start a family*.

    A. get married　　　　　B. get divorced　　　　　C. have children

(　　) 15. She described her husband as a man with a *friendly* face when they met for the first time.

    A. harmonious　　　　　B. ugly　　　　　C. pleasant

✓ FILLING THE BLANKS

housewife;　marry;　private;　childhood;　surname;
marriage;　bride;　honeymoon;　teenagers;　trust;
anniversary;　middle-aged;　neighbour;　babysit;　parents

1. Can you show me how to spell your _____?

2. In a good _____, both husband and wife are supposed to work hard to solve any arising problem.

3. Our next-door _____ moved in last year. They are very noisy.

4. This fashion magazine aims at _____ between the ages of 15 and 19.

5. The year 2019 witnesses the 70th _____ of the founding of the People's Republic of China.

6. She asked me to _____ her four-month-old son.

7. Jeremy constructed this story from the memories of his _____.

8. The first time I went abroad was on my _____ with my husband in Paris.

9. When she arrived, she found that there were only some _____, married businessmen instead of single handsome boys in the party.

10. My sister is getting _____ on Sunday.

11. Martha changed schools from a small _____ school to a public school.

12. The _____ and groom toasted the coming guests with champagne.

13. _____ should not spoil their children and promise easily.

14. Cinthia became a traditional _____ and mother of three children after marrying a merchant prince.

15. The basic of a good marriage is _____.Otherwise, the two will quarrel over trifles every day.

☑ SPEAKING

1. **Tell me something about your best friend.**
2. **Tell me something about your family.**

CHECK

1. guest _____   2. parent _____   3. husband _____

4. 青少年 _____   5. 长大 _____   6. 已婚的 _____

7. neighbour _____   8. surname _____   9. wife _____

10. 童年 _____   11. 临时保姆 _____   12. 蜜月 _____

13. bride _____   14. bridegroom _____   15. trust _____

16. 中年的 _____   17. 私有的 _____   18. 怀孕的 _____

19. niece _____   20. nephew _____

Day **7** *House and Home* 房屋与住所

VOCABULARY

 基础词汇

词汇		词义	默写
address /əˈdres/	*n.*	地址	
apartment /əˈpɑːtmənt/	*n.*	公寓套房	
armchair /ˈɑːmtʃeə(r)/	*n.*	扶手椅	
bathtub /ˈbɑːθtʌb/	*n.*	浴缸	
bathroom /ˈbɑːθruːm/	*n.*	浴室	
bedroom /ˈbedruːm/	*n.*	卧室	
bin /bɪn/	*n.*	（有盖）大容器，箱，柜	
blanket /ˈblæŋkɪt/	*n.*	毯子；毛毯	
bookcase /ˈbʊkkeɪs/	*n.*	书柜	
bookshelf /ˈbʊkʃelf/	*n.*	书架	
bowl /bəʊl/	*n.*	碗	
carpet /ˈkɑːpɪt/	*n.*	地毯	
cooker /ˈkʊkə(r)/	*n.*	厨灶；炉具	
cupboard /ˈkʌbəd/	*n.*	橱柜	
curtain /ˈkɜːtn/	*n.*	窗帘	
dining room	*n.*	餐厅	
downstairs /ˌdaʊnˈsteəz/	*adv.*	在楼下；往楼下	
drawer /drɔː(r)/	*n.*	抽屉	
entrance /ˈentrəns/	*n.*	入口（处）	
flat /flæt/	*n.*	公寓	

fridge /frɪdʒ/	n.	冰箱
furniture /ˈfɜːnɪtʃə(r)/	n.	家具
garage /ˈɡærɑːʒ/	n.	车库
garden /ˈɡɑːdn/	n.	花园
gas /ɡæs/	n.	天然气；气体
gate /ɡeɪt/	n.	大门
hall /hɔːl/	n.	大厅
heating /ˈhiːtɪŋ/	n.	暖气设备；供暖系统
home /həʊm/	n.	家；住所
house /haʊs/	n.	房屋；房子
key /kiː/	n.	钥匙；关键
kitchen /ˈkɪtʃɪn/	n.	厨房
lamp /læmp/	n.	灯
oven /ˈʌvn/	n.	烤箱
pillow /ˈpɪləʊ/	n.	枕头
refrigerator /rɪˈfrɪdʒəreɪtə(r)/	n.	冰箱
roof /ruːf/	n.	顶部；屋顶；车顶
rubbish /ˈrʌbɪʃ/	n.	垃圾
safe /seɪf/	adj.	安全的
shelf /ʃelf/	n.	架子；搁板
shower /ˈʃaʊə(r)/	n.	淋浴
sink /sɪŋk/	n.	洗涤池；洗碗槽
sitting room	n.	客厅
sofa /ˈsəʊfə/	n.	长沙发
stay /steɪ/	v.	停留
tidy /ˈtaɪdi/	adj.	整洁的 v. 使整洁
tidy up		整理
toilet /ˈtɔɪlət/	n.	厕所

✅ 重点词汇

词 汇		词 义	默写
accommodation /əˌkɒməˈdeɪʃn/	*n.*	住处；停留处；办公处	
air conditioner	*n.*	空调机	
alarm clock	*n.*	闹钟	
antique /ænˈtiːk/	*n.*	古董	
balcony /ˈbælkəni/	*n.*	阳台	
basin /ˈbeɪsn/	*n.*	盆；调菜盆	
blind /blaɪnd/	*n.*	卷帘 *adj.* 失明的	
block /blɒk/	*n.*	街区	
bucket /ˈbʌkɪt/	*n.*	（有提梁的）桶	
bulb /bʌlb/	*n.*	电灯泡	
candle /ˈkændl/	*n.*	蜡烛	
ceiling /ˈsiːlɪŋ/	*n.*	天花板	
cellar /ˈselə(r)/	*n.*	地窖	
central heating	*n.*	集中供热	
chest of drawers	*n.*	（有抽屉的）衣橱	
cottage /ˈkɒtɪdʒ/	*n.*	小屋	
cushion /ˈkʊʃn/	*n.*	软垫；坐垫；靠垫	
decorate /ˈdekəreɪt/	*v.*	装饰	
decoration /ˌdekəˈreɪʃn/	*n.*	装饰；装饰品	
dishwasher /ˈdɪʃwɒʃə(r)/	*n.*	洗碗碟机	
dustbin /ˈdʌstbɪn/	*n.*	垃圾桶；垃圾箱	
duvet /ˈduːveɪ/	*n.*	羽绒被	
flatmate /ˈflætmeɪt/	*n.*	室友；合住公寓套间者	
freezer /ˈfriːzə(r)/	*n.*	冷冻柜	
frying pan	*n.*	长柄平底煎锅	
handle /ˈhændl/	*n.*	把手；柄 *v.* 处理；应付	
handkerchief /ˈhæŋkətʃɪf/	*n.*	手帕；纸巾	

heater /ˈhiːtə(r)/	n.	加热器；炉子；热水器
hi-fi /ˈhaɪ faɪ/	n.	高保真音响设备
iron /ˈaɪən/	n.	熨斗 v. 熨；烫平
kettle /ˈketl/	n.	（烧水用的）壶，水壶
ladder /ˈlædə(r)/	n.	梯子；阶梯；途径
microwave /ˈmaɪkrəweɪv/	n.	微波炉
pipe /paɪp/	n.	管子
plug /plʌg/	n.	插头
plug in		接通（电源）；把（插头）插进（插座）
pot /pɒt/	n.	锅
property /ˈprɒpəti/	n.	财产；所有物
remote control	n.	遥控
saucepan /ˈsɔːspən/	n.	深煮锅
step /step/	n.	台阶；步伐；阶段
surround /səˈraʊnd/	v.	环绕
vase /vɑːz/	n.	花瓶

✅ 进阶加油站

◆ 构词法小知识

名词后缀	示 例	
-er （-er 除了可以表示人，还可以表示物）	**heater**	加热器
	dishwasher	洗碗碟机
	freezer	冷冻柜
	cooker	厨灶；炉具
	drawer	抽屉

EXERCISE

✓ MATCH

(   ) 1. cooker

(   ) 2. pillow

(   ) 3. blanket

(   ) 4. roof

(   ) 5. bookshelf

(   ) 6. fridge

(   ) 7. drawer

(   ) 8. garage

(   ) 9. kettle

(   ) 10. heater

(   ) 11. decorate

(   ) 12. remote control

(   ) 13. air conditioner

(   ) 14. basin

(   ) 15. handkerchief

(   ) 16. bathroom

(   ) 17. armchair

(   ) 18. sitting room

a. the ability to operate a machine from a distance using radio or electrical signals

b. a square or rectangular piece of cloth filled with soft material, used to rest your head on in bed

c. to make sth. look more attractive by putting things on it

d. a machine used for making air or water warmer

e. a small piece of material or paper that you use for blowing your nose, etc.

f. a building for keeping one or more cars or other vehicles in

g. a machine that cools and dries air

h. a large piece of equipment for cooking food, containing an oven and gas or electric rings on top

i. a shelf that you keep books on

j. a large cover, often made of wool, used especially on beds to keep people warm

k. a large round bowl for holding liquids or for preparing foods in

l. a part of a piece of furniture such as a desk, used for keeping things in

m. a comfortable chair with sides on which you can rest your arms

n. the structure that covers or forms the top of a building or vehicle

o. a room in a house where people sit together, watch television, etc.

p. a room in which there is a bath, a washbasin and often a toilet

q. a container with a lid, handle and a spout, used for boiling water

r. a piece of electrical equipment in which food is kept cold so that it stays fresh

✅ MULTIPLE CHOICES

( ) 1. I'll explain it to you *step by step*.

    A. quickly   B. gradually   C. generally

( ) 2. I started helping him do housework when he *went blind*.

    A. was hurt   B. went mad   C. wasn't able to see

( ) 3. The rain was coming up *in buckets*.

    A. heavily   B. slowly   C. loudly

( ) 4. They used to live in a *cottage* in the northwest of Suzhou.

    A. small house   B. village   C. town

( ) 5. To be honest, I doubt whether Jacob can *handle* the job.

    A. operate   B. change   C. cope with

( ) 6. Jack was thrown out of a side *entrance* with his hand covering his wound.

    A. door   B. inside   C. exit

( ) 7. That is totally a new building without any *decoration*.

    A. dressing   B. adornment   C. make-up

( ) 8. If you want to *get the ladder of success*, you should prepare yourself every day.

    A. climb up

    B. approach success

    C. drop down

( ) 9. It is reported that a bomb exploded in a *dustbin* last Friday.

    A. garbage can   B. rubbish collector   C. garbage room

( ) 10. Ms. Jones had to *tidy up* her kid's room.

    A. set out   B. clean up   C. run out

( ) 11. The valley is *surrounded* by forests.

    A. enclosed   B. embraced   C. separated

( ) 12. These three buildings are government *property*.

    A. possessions   B. decoration   C. furniture

( ) 13. The *key* to success is preparation.

    A. essential factor

    B. the least important factor

C. unconsidered factor

(   ) 14. He switched on the bedside *lamp* and went to the bathroom.

    A. lamb   B. beam   C. light

☑ FILLING THE BLANKS

curtains;	safe;	tidying up;	candle;	blocks;
antique;	ceilings;	bathroom;	refrigerator;	heating;
downstairs;	address;	flatmate;	rubbish;	carpet

1. I found a genuine _____ in the attic（阁楼）of our old house.

2. We lit a single _____ in the living room after the power cut.

3. He walked four _____ down Green Street to find a cab.

4. I am satisfied with those spacious rooms with tall windows and high _____.

5. I had a fierce quarrel with my _____ because he used my dishwasher without my permission.

6. I'll give you my _____ and phone number, so you can contact me whenever you want.

7. Denise went _____ and served the guest with some tea.

8. Jane spent the whole day cleaning and _____.

9. The stadium was dirty and littered with _____ after the vocal concert.

10. Parents should tell their children that the street is not _____ for them to play in.

11. Jasmine and Wilson laid a new _____ on the top of wooden boards.

12. She draws her bedroom _____ every day to keep out the sunlight.

13. My bedroom has its own _____, so I can take a shower in my own room.

14. The sashimi（刺身）can be served straight from the _____.

15. They are too poor, so they are considering to reduce the cost of _____ and air-conditioning.

✓ SPEAKING

Here is a photograph. It shows a beautiful room. Talk on your own about the photograph for one minute.

 **CHECK**

1. bathroom _____   2. entrance _____   3. furniture _____

4. 浴缸 _____   5. 抽屉 _____   6. 橱柜 _____

7. lamp _____   8. roof _____   9. rubbish _____

10. 长沙发 _____   11. 整洁的 _____   12. 阳台 _____

13. bulb _____   14. ceiling _____   15. cottage _____

16. （有提梁的）桶 ____   17. 垃圾箱 _____   18. 熨斗 _____

19. plug _____   20. property _____

Day **8** *Health, Medicine and Exercise*
健康、医疗与锻炼

VOCABULARY

✅ 基础词汇

词　汇	词　义	默写
accident /ˈæksɪdənt/	*n.* （交通）事故；意外遭遇	
ambulance /ˈæmbjələns/	*n.* 救护车	
appointment /əˈpɔɪntmənt/	*n.* 预约	
brain /breɪn/	*n.* 脑	
chemist /ˈkemɪst/	*n.* 药剂师	
cold /kəʊld/	*n.* 感冒	
	adj. 寒冷的	
danger /ˈdeɪndʒə(r)/	*n.* 危险；危害	
dangerous /ˈdeɪndʒərəs/	*adj.* 有危险的	
dead /ded/	*adj.* 死的；不运行的	
dentist /ˈdentɪst/	*n.* 牙科医生	
die /daɪ/	*v.* 死亡	
doctor /ˈdɒktə(r)/	*n.* 医生	
drugstore /ˈdrʌgstɔː(r)/	*n.* 药店	
exercise /ˈeksəsaɪz/	*n.* 运动；锻炼	
earache /ˈɪəreɪk/	*n.* 耳痛	
finger /ˈfɪŋgə(r)/	*n.* 手指	

fit /fɪt/	*adj.*	健康的；健壮的
hair /heə(r)/	*n.*	头发
headache /ˈhedeɪk/	*n.*	头痛
health /helθ/	*n.*	健康
hear /hɪə(r)/	*v.*	听到
heart /hɑːt/	*n.*	心
hospital /ˈhɒspɪtl/	*n.*	医院
ill /ɪl/	*adj.*	有病；不舒服
lie down		躺下
medicine /ˈmedsn/	*n.*	药；医学；医疗
nose /nəʊz/	*n.*	鼻子
nurse /nɜːs/	*n.*	护士
pain /peɪn/	*n.*	（身体上的）疼痛
pale /peɪl/	*adj.*	苍白的
sick /sɪk/	*adj.*	生病的
stomach /ˈstʌmək/	*n.*	胃
stomach ache	*n.*	胃痛
temperature /ˈtemprətʃə(r)/	*n.*	温度；气温；体温
tired /ˈtaɪəd/	*adj.*	疲倦的
tooth /tuːθ/	*n.*	牙齿
toothache /ˈtuːθeɪk/	*n.*	牙痛
toothbrush /ˈtuːθbrʌʃ/	*n.*	牙刷

✅ 重点词汇

词汇		词义	默写
ankle /ˈæŋkl/	*n.*	踝关节	
aspirin /ˈæsprɪn/	*n.*	阿司匹林	
bandage /ˈbændɪdʒ/	*n.*	绷带	

bleed /bliːd/	*v.*	流血
bone /bəʊn/	*n.*	骨头
breath /breθ/	*n.*	呼吸的空气
breathe /briːð/	*v.*	呼吸
bite /baɪt/	*v.*	咬；叮
chin /tʃɪn/	*n.*	下巴
cough /kɒf/	*v./n.*	咳嗽
damage /ˈdæmɪdʒ/	*n.*	损坏；损失；损害
deaf /def/	*adj.*	聋的
elbow /ˈelbəʊ/	*n.*	肘部
emergency /iˈmɜːdʒənsi/	*n.*	突发事件；紧急情况
fever /ˈfiːvə(r)/	*n.*	发烧
flu /fluː/	*n.*	流感
heel /hiːl/	*n.*	脚后跟
herb /hɜːb/	*n.*	草本；药草；香草
injure /ˈɪndʒə(r)/	*v.*	伤害；使受伤
keep fit		保持健康
knee /niː/	*n.*	膝盖
operation /ˌɒpəˈreɪʃn/	*n.*	手术
painful /ˈpeɪnfl/	*adj.*	令人疼痛的
patient /ˈpeɪʃnt/	*n.*	病人
pharmacy /ˈfɑːməsi/	*n.*	药房
pill /pɪl/	*n.*	药丸
prescription /prɪˈskrɪpʃn/	*n.*	处方
recover /rɪˈkʌvə(r)/	*v.*	恢复健康；康复
severe /sɪˈvɪə(r)/	*adj.*	极为恶劣的；十分严重的
shoulder /ˈʃəʊldə(r)/	*n.*	肩膀
skin /skɪn/	*n.*	皮肤
sore throat	*n.*	喉咙痛
stress /stres/	*n.*	压力
tablet /ˈtæblət/	*n.*	药片
thumb /θʌm/	*n.*	拇指

✓ 进阶加油站

◆ 高频短语

a high fever	发烧	a runny nose	流鼻涕
a sore throat	嗓子疼	an infectious disease	传染病
a routine check	例行检查	severe symptom	严重的症状
be allergic to sth.	对……过敏	take medicine	吃药
have an injection	打针		

◆ 构词法小知识

由两个或两个以上的词合成一个新词，这种构词法叫作**合成法**，常见的有复合名词、复合动词、复合形容词等。

- 复合名词

    名词 + 名词：**boyfriend, girlfriend, bridegroom, housewife, honeymoon，toothbrush, toothpaste**

    名词 + 动词：**toothache, headache, stomachache, backache**

    名词 + 动词 -ing 形式：**babysitting**

- 复合动词

    名词 + 动词：**babysit, sunbathe**

- 复合形容词

    形容词 + 分词：**middle-aged, new-born**

EXERCISE

☑ MATCH

( ) 1. chemist	a. having skin that is almost white
( ) 2. cold	b. a medical condition in which a person has a temperature that is higher than normal
( ) 3. dentist	c. a small brush for cleaning your teeth
( ) 4. earache	d. a person whose job is to take care of sick or injured people, usually in a hospital
( ) 5. stomach	e. a common illness that affects the nose and/or throat, making you cough, sneeze , etc.
( ) 6. pale	f. to lose blood, especially from a wound or an injury
( ) 7. toothbrush	g. a drug used to reduce pain, fever and inflammation
( ) 8. aspirin	h. a person whose job is to take care of people's teeth
( ) 9. bleed	i. a continuous pain in the head
( ) 10. breath	j. the air that you take into your lungs and send out again
( ) 11. deaf	k. a plant whose leaves, flowers or seeds are used to flavour food, in medicines or for their pleasant smell
( ) 12. fever	l. a person whose job is to prepare and sell medicines, and who works in a shop
( ) 13. herb	m. the joint between the upper and lower parts of the arm where it bends in the middle
( ) 14. pill	n. the short thick finger at the side of the hand, slightly apart from the other four
( ) 15. skin	o. a substance, especially a liquid that you drink or swallow in order to cure an illness
( ) 16. thumb	p. the layer of tissue that covers the body
( ) 17. headache	q. pain inside the ear
( ) 18. medicine	r. a small flat round piece of medicine that you swallow without chewing it
( ) 19. nurse	s. the organ inside the body where food goes when you swallow it
( ) 20. elbow	t. unable to hear anything or unable to hear very well

✅ MULTIPLE CHOICES

( ) 1. James is *recovering* from the illness.

　　A. becoming well 　　　　B. returning 　　　　C. repairing

( ) 2. The flood caused *damage* to the local people.

　　A. conflict 　　　　B. physical harm 　　　　C. pressure

( ) 3. Jane can always deal with *emergencies* promptly.

　　A. unexpected situations 　　B. worries 　　　　C. anxieties

( ) 4. Katy has been under *stress* since she started to work.

　　A. pressure 　　　　B. relief 　　　　C. importance

( ) 5. That is a very *dangerous* bridge. Don't go there!

　　A. severe 　　　　B. serious 　　　　C. unsafe

( ) 6. Unfortunately, both Luna's father and mother *died* when she was only six years old.

　　A. passed away 　　　　B. disappeared 　　　　C. vanished

( ) 7. You need to give your upper body *an exercise* with weights (哑铃).

　　A. a sport 　　　　B. a workout 　　　　C. a movement

( ) 8. An averagely *healthy* person can master easy swimming skills within three days.

　　A. proper 　　　　B. suitable 　　　　C. fit

( ) 9. Vivian was suffering from a *sharp* pain in her ankle.

　　A. severe 　　　　B. moderate 　　　　C. light

( ) 10. Micheal is very *sick*. He needs doctor's prescription and buys some medication.

　　A. dizzy 　　　　B. unbalanced 　　　　C. ill

( ) 11. Who called the *ambulance* just now?

　　A. vehicle taking people to a hospital

　　B. vehicle taking people to a hotel

　　C. vehicle taking people to a restaurant

( ) 12. A number of bombs have exploded last week, seriously *injuring* at least nine people.

　　A. ruining 　　　　B. wounding 　　　　C. offending

( ) 13. The hospital leader promises the patient that they will schedule the *operation* as

　　soon as possible.

　　A. surgery 　　　　B. procedure 　　　　C. process

( ) 14. The battery is *dead*. You can replace it with a new one.

    A. no longer living

    B. having no energy

    C. having no living creatures

( ) 15. Please help me pick up this medicine from the *pharmacy*.

    A. drugstore   B. hospital   C. drug administration

☑ FILLING THE BLANKS

ankle;	accidents;	breathing;	appointment;	dangers;
keep fit;	bitten;	temperature;	flu;	tired;
coughed;	prescription;	ambulance;	bandage;	hospital

1. I've got a dental _____ at 2 o'clock this afternoon, so can we meet after 6 p.m.?

2. We put a _____ on his wounded knee to stop it from bleeding.

3. She stood there _____ deeply and felt relaxed.

4. Graham _____ violently last night, and his roommates could not sleep at all.

5. I got _____, so please stay away from me in case you are infected.

6. It is weird that she was _____ by her family dog.

7. One of the best ways to _____ is to jog for 30 minutes every day.

8. It is a common sense that sleeping pills are only available by _____.

9. I twisted my _____ badly, so the doctor suggested me to lie in bed for a week.

10. 500,000 people die every year because of car _____.

11. This advertisement shows the _____ of smoking for teenagers.

12. The injured in this accident were sent to the nearest _____ in an ambulance.

13. Olivia began to run an extremely high _____.

14. The sick child was sent to hospital by _____.

15. She's too _____ even to talk, so let's leave her alone to make her have a good sleep.

 **READING**

Questions 1-6

For each question, choose the correct answer.

A cold is known as the common cold for a reason, which is the most frequent infectious disease in humans. The 1 _____ adult suffers from a cold two to four times a year. Children often get between five and seven colds a year due to their 2 _____ contact with other children. The symptoms of a cold are a 3 _____ throat and a runny nose. Although colds are usually relatively mild, they are a 4 _____ cause of doctor visits and absences from school and work. See your doctor if you have a 5 _____ fever or muscle aches. More 6 _____ symptoms may mean you have flu instead.

1. A. common	B. general	C. average	D. ordinary
2. A. close	B. near	C. nearby	D. far
3. A. pain	B. severe	C. sore	D. painful
4. A. real	B. main	C. fact	D. true
5. A. high	B. sharp	C. deep	D. low
6. A. heavy	B. serious	C. strong	D. severe

 **CHECK**

1. ambulance _____   2. drugstore _____   3. nurse _____

4. 预约 _____   5. 牙科医生 _____   6. 头痛 _____

7. pale _____   8. medicine _____   9. sore throat _____

10. 流血 _____   11. 咳嗽 _____   12. 聋的 _____

13. stomach ache _____   14. operation _____   15. pharmacy _____

16. 药丸 _____   17. 恢复健康 _____   18. 压力 _____

19. flu _____   20. tablet _____

Day ⑨ *Food and Drink* 食物与饮品

 VOCABULARY

✅ 基础词汇

词 汇		词 义	默写
biscuit /ˈbɪskɪt/	*n.*	饼干	
boil /bɔɪl/	*v.*	煮	
breakfast /ˈbrekfəst/	*n.*	早餐	
burger /ˈbɜːgə(r)/	*n.*	汉堡包	
butter /ˈbʌtə(r)/	*n.*	黄油	
cafeteria /ˌkæfəˈtɪəriə/	*n.*	自助餐厅	
candy /ˈkændi/	*n.*	糖果	
carrot /ˈkærət/	*n.*	胡萝卜	
cereal /ˈsɪəriəl/	*n.*	谷类食物	
cheese /tʃiːz/	*n.*	奶酪	
chilli /ˈtʃɪli/	*n.*	辣椒	
chip /tʃɪp/	*n.*	炸薯条	
chocolate /ˈtʃɒklət/	*n.*	巧克力	
coffee /ˈkɒfi/	*n.*	咖啡	
cola /ˈkəʊlə/	*n.*	可乐饮料	
cook /kʊk/	*v.*	烹饪	
cream /kriːm/	*n.*	奶油	
curry /ˈkʌri/	*n.*	咖喱菜	
delicious /dɪˈlɪʃəs/	*adj.*	美味的	

dessert /dɪˈzɜːt/	*n.*	甜点
dinner /ˈdɪnə(r)/	*n.*	主餐；正餐
fruit /fruːt/	*n.*	水果
garlic /ˈɡɑːlɪk/	*n.*	大蒜
grape /ɡreɪp/	*n.*	葡萄
grill /ɡrɪl/	*v.*	烧烤；炙烤
honey /ˈhʌni/	*n.*	蜂蜜
hungry /ˈhʌŋɡri/	*adj.*	饥饿的；渴望的
ice cream	*n.*	冰淇淋；冰激凌
jam /dʒæm/	*n.*	果酱
juice /dʒuːs/	*n.*	果汁
lemon /ˈlemən/	*n.*	柠檬
lemonade /ˌleməˈneɪd/	*n.*	柠檬味汽水
lunch /lʌntʃ/	*n.*	午餐
main course	*n.*	主菜
melon /ˈmelən/	*n.*	甜瓜；瓜
menu /ˈmenjuː/	*n.*	菜单
mineral water	*n.*	矿泉水
mushroom /ˈmʌʃrʊm/	*n.*	蘑菇
oil /ɔɪl/	*n.*	食用油
omelette /ˈɒmlət/	*n.*	煎蛋卷；摊鸡蛋；鸡蛋饼
onion /ˈʌnjən/	*n.*	洋葱
pasta /ˈpæstə/	*n.*	意大利面
pepper /ˈpepə(r)/	*n.*	胡椒粉
picnic /ˈpɪknɪk/	*n.*	野餐
pizza /ˈpiːtsə/	*n.*	比萨饼
potato /pəˈteɪtəʊ/	*n.*	马铃薯；土豆
roast /rəʊst/	*v.*	烤
salad /ˈsæləd/	*n.*	蔬菜沙拉
yogurt /ˈjɒɡət/	*n.*	酸奶

salt /sɔːlt/	*n.*	盐
sandwich /ˈsænwɪtʃ/	*n.*	三明治
sauce /sɔːs/	*n.*	酱
sausage /ˈsɒsɪdʒ/	*n.*	香肠
soup /suːp/	*n.*	汤
steak /steɪk/	*n.*	牛排
strawberry /ˈstrɔːbəri/	*n.*	草莓
sugar /ˈʃʊɡə(r)/	*n.*	糖
thirsty /ˈθɜːsti/	*adj.*	口渴的
toast /təʊst/	*n.*	烤面包片；吐司；祝酒
tomato /təˈmɑːtəʊ/	*n.*	番茄

☑ 重点词汇

词汇	词义		默写
bake /beɪk/	*v.*	烘烤；焙	
barbecue /ˈbɑːbɪkjuː/	*n.*	户外烧烤	
bitter /ˈbɪtə(r)/	*adj.*	味苦的	
broccoli /ˈbrɒkəli/	*n.*	西兰花	
cabbage /ˈkæbɪdʒ/	*n.*	卷心菜	
canteen /kænˈtiːn/	*n.*	食堂；餐厅	
chewing gum	*n.*	口香糖	
coconut /ˈkəʊkənʌt/	*n.*	椰子	
corn /kɔːn/	*n.*	玉米；谷物	
cucumber /ˈkjuːkʌmbə(r)/	*n.*	黄瓜	
diet /ˈdaɪət/	*n.*	日常饮食；规定饮食	
flavour /ˈfleɪvə(r)/	*n.*	味道	
flour /ˈflaʊə(r)/	*n.*	面粉	
French fry	*n.*	炸薯条	
fry /fraɪ/	*v.*	油炸	

grill /grɪl/	*n.*	烤架
ingredient /ɪnˈgriːdiənt/	*n.*	成分；（尤指烹饪）材料
lamb /læm/	*n.*	羔羊
lettuce /ˈletɪs/	*n.*	生菜
peanut /ˈpiːnʌt/	*n.*	花生
pineapple /ˈpaɪnæpl/	*n.*	菠萝
raw meat	*n.*	生肉
recipe /ˈresəpi/	*n.*	食谱
refreshments /rɪˈfreʃmənts/	*n.*	饮料；小食
roll /rəʊl/	*n.*	小面包条
salmon /ˈsæmən/	*n.*	鲑；大麻哈鱼
soft drink	*n.*	软饮料
sour /ˈsaʊə(r)/	*adj.*	酸的
spicy /ˈspaɪsi/	*adj.*	辛辣的
spinach /ˈspɪnɪtʃ/	*n.*	菠菜
takeaway /ˈteɪkəweɪ/	*n.*	外卖食物；外卖餐馆
tasty /ˈteɪsti/	*adj.*	美味的
turkey /ˈtɜːki/	*n.*	火鸡
tuna /ˈtjuːnə/	*n.*	金枪鱼
vegetarian /ˌvedʒəˈteəriən/	*n.*	素食者

✓ 进阶加油站

◆ 形容食物与饮品的量词短语

a bunch of bananas/grapes	一串香蕉 / 葡萄	a piece of cake	一块蛋糕
a bowl of rice	一碗米饭	a handful of rice/corn	一把大米 / 玉米
a slice of bread	一片面包	a bag of peanuts	一包花生
a loaf of bread	一条面包	a bar of chocolate	一块巧克力
a spoonful of sugar	一勺糖	a glass of lemonade	一杯柠檬水

EXERCISE

☑ MATCH

( ) 1. butter

( ) 2. peanut

( ) 3. sausage

( ) 4. omelette

( ) 5. cafeteria

( ) 6. dessert

( ) 7. lemonade

( ) 8. picnic

( ) 9. yogurt

( ) 10. steak

( ) 11. bitter

( ) 12. sauce

( ) 13. tasty

( ) 14. chocolate

( ) 15. curry

( ) 16. garlic

( ) 17. mineral water

( ) 18. lettuce

a. sweet food eaten at the end of a meal

b. having a strong, unpleasant taste; not sweet

c. water from a spring in the ground that contains mineral salts or gases

d. a sweet fizzy drink with a lemon flavour

e. a nut that grows underground in a thin shell

f. a vegetable of the onion family with a very strong taste and smell, used in cooking to give flavour to food

g. a restaurant where you choose and pay for your meal at a counter and carry it to a table

h. a thick liquid that is eaten with food to add flavour to it

i. a mixture of finely chopped meat, fat, bread, etc. in a long tube of skin, cooked and eaten whole or served cold in thin slices

j. a hot dish of eggs mixed together and fried, often with cheese, meat, vegetables, etc. added

k. having a strong and pleasant flavour

l. an occasion when people pack a meal and take it to eat outdoors, especially in the countryside

m. a thick slice of good quality beef

n. a South Asian dish of meat, vegetables, etc. cooked with hot spices, often served with rice

o. a thick white liquid food, made by adding bacteria to milk, served cold and often flavoured with fruit

p. a soft yellow food made from cream, used in cooking and for spreading on bread

q. a hard brown sweet food made from cocoa beans , used in cooking to add flavour to cakes, etc. or eaten as a sweet/candy

r. a plant with large green leaves that are eaten raw, especially in salad

☑ *MULTIPLE CHOICES*

(   ) 1. Let's have a *takeaway* tonight.

A. takeout   B. takein   C. takefrom

(   ) 2. Do you know whether she is *a vegetarian* or not?

A. a person who eats either vegetables or meat

B. a person who eat only fruit

C. a person who doesn't eat meat or fish

(   ) 3. She *is on a diet* recently, so that she can show her excellent figure in her wedding ceremony.

A. is eating less food than usual

B. makes her recipe

C. is getting weight

(   ) 4. Thank you so much for this *tasty* meal.

A. colorful   B. juicy   C. delicious

(   ) 5. This kind of leaves they eat every day taste rather *bitter*.

A. sweet   B. not sweet   C. pleasant

(   ) 6. The tomatoes give extra *flavour* to the soup.

A. fragrance   B. smell   C. taste

(   ) 7. You can find all sorts of sweet and *spicy* food in that restaurant.

A. hot   B. sour   C. bitter

(   ) 8. Having a bottle of *soft drink* is not enough to quench my thirst.

A. non-alcoholic beverage

B. coco cola

C. mineral water

(   ) 9. We all know that Louis is *hungry for* success.

A. looking out   B. thirsty for   C. searching

(   ) 10. No dessert, please. It is totally enough for me to finish *the main course*.

A. the main class

B. the principal dish of the meal

C. all the food

(   ) 11. I will go to the bookshop to buy a *recipe book*.

       A. menu   B. cookbook   C. notebook

(   ) 12. As soon as I arrived at the restaurant, a waiter offered me the *menu*.

       A. specialties   B. list of dishes available   C. bill

(   ) 13. I personally would rather *roast* a chicken in the holiday.

       A. bake   B. cook by dry heat   C. fry

(   ) 14. Lara is basting the leg of *lamb* and Jasmine is preparing lettuce for us.

       A. a young sheep   B. a young cow   C. a young pig

✓ FILLING THE BLANKS

carrots;	toast;	honey;	sweet;	thirsty;
fried;	barbecue;	turkeys;	boiled;	breakfast;
bake;	salty;	recipe;	sugar	

1. My wife and I drank a _____ to the bride and groom.

2. Conventional instant noodles require _____ water, but self-heating foods such as rice and hotpot dishes can be heated up after opening via a chemical reaction, or after simply adding tap water.

3. Do you want milk and eggs for _____?

4. Jiaxing zongzi is well known for its typical filling of marinated pork which is neither too _____ nor too sweet, satisfying the palates of the majority.

5. _____ the cakes for 35 to 50 minutes, and serve the guests with these cakes in our party.

6. On New Year's Eve, our family had a _____ in our backyard.

7. She would improve her diet if she ate less _____ food and snacked less.

8. In the US, people usually eat _____ at Thanksgiving.

9. This cherry has a purple-red appearance and thick skin. Its texture is soft and juicy with a _____ and sour flavor.

10. You'd better drink enough water in case you feel _____ in the half way.

11. Drinking water with _____ can help to relieve your sore throat.

12. According to a recent report, eating _____ benefits your eyes.

13. When I drink coffee, I would add some _____, so it won't taste too bitter.

14. This _____ can tell you the ingredients you need to make curry rice.

SPEAKING

1. **What kind of food do you like most?**
2. **Do you have a balanced diet?**

CHECK

1. biscuit _____

2. butter _____

3. grape _____

4. 果汁 _____

5. 蘑菇 _____

6. 柠檬 _____

7. sausage _____

8. carrot _____

9. melon _____

10. 甜点 _____

11. 柠檬味汽水 _____

12. 汤 _____

13. broccoli _____

14. coconut _____

15. flour _____

16. 油炸 _____

17. 外卖食物 _____

18. 辛辣的 _____

19. recipe _____

20. peanut _____

Day ⑩ Clothes and Accessories

服装与配饰

VOCABULARY

✅ 基础词汇

词 汇		词 义	默 写
belt /belt/	*n.*	腰带	
blouse /blaʊz/	*n.*	（女士）衬衫	
boot /buːt/	*n.*	靴子	
bracelet /ˈbreɪslət/	*n.*	手镯；手链	
cap /kæp/	*n.*	便帽；制服帽	
chain /tʃeɪn/	*n.*	链子	
coat /kəʊt/	*n.*	外套	
dress /dres/	*n.*	连衣裙	
earring /ˈɪərɪŋ/	*n.*	耳环	
fashion /ˈfæʃn/	*n.*	时尚	
get dressed		穿好衣服	
glasses /ˈglɑːsɪz/	*n.*	眼镜	
glove /glʌv/	*n.*	（分手指的）手套	
handbag /ˈhændbæg/	*n.*	（女士）手提包	
jacket /ˈdʒækɪt/	*n.*	夹克衫	
jeans /dʒiːnz/	*n.*	牛仔裤	

jewellery /ˈdʒuːəlri/	n.	珠宝；首饰
jumper /ˈdʒʌmpə(r)/	n.	针织套衫
necklace /ˈnekləs/	n.	项链
purse /pɜːs/	n.	（女士）钱包
pocket /ˈpɒkɪt/	n.	口袋
raincoat /ˈreɪnkəʊt/	n.	雨衣
ring /rɪŋ/	n.	戒指
scarf /skɑːf/	n.	围巾
shirt /ʃɜːt/	n.	衬衫
shorts /ʃɔːts/	n.	短裤
skirt /skɜːt/	n.	裙子
suit /suːt/	n.	西装；套装
sunglasses /ˈsʌnglɑːsɪz/	n.	太阳镜
sweater /ˈswetə(r)/	n.	毛衣
swimming costume	n.	游泳衣
swimsuit /ˈswɪmsuːt/	n.	游泳衣
tie /taɪ/	n.	领带
	v.	（用线、绳等）系，拴，绑
tights /taɪts/	n.	（女用）连裤袜，紧身裤
trainer /ˈtreɪnə(r)/	n.	运动鞋
trousers /ˈtraʊzəz/	n.	裤子
T-shirt /ˈtiː ʃɜːt/	n.	T 恤衫
uniform /ˈjuːnɪfɔːm/	n.	制服；校服
wallet /ˈwɒlɪt/	n.	钱包
watch /wɒtʃ/	n.	手表

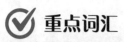 **重点词汇**

词汇		词义	默写
brand /brænd/	*n.*	品牌	
buyer /'baɪə(r)/	*n.*	买主	
collar /'kɒlə(r)/	*n.*	衣领；领子；颈圈	
cotton /'kɒtn/	*n.*	棉花；棉布	
fashionable /'fæʃnəbl/	*adj.*	流行的；时髦的	
fasten /'fɑːsn/	*v.*	系牢；扎牢	
fold /fəʊld/	*v.*	折叠	
handkerchief /'hæŋkətʃɪf/	*n.*	手帕；纸巾	
knit /nɪt/	*v.*	编织；（使）愈合，接合	
label /'leɪbl/	*n.*	标签；签条	
laundry /'lɔːndri/	*n.*	洗衣店；洗衣房	
leather /'leðə(r)/	*n.*	皮革	
logo /'ləʊgəʊ/	*n.*	标识；标志	
make-up /'meɪk ʌp/	*n.*	化妆品	
match /mætʃ/	*v.*	般配；相配	
	n.	比赛；竞赛	
material /mə'tɪəriəl/	*n.*	布料；材料	
old-fashioned	*adj.*	过时的；陈旧的；保守的	
pattern /'pætn/	*n.*	图案；花样；式样	
perfume /'pɜːfjuːm/	*n.*	香水；芳香；香味	
plastic /'plæstɪk/	*n.*	塑料	
pullover /'pʊləʊvə(r)/	*n.*	套头毛衣；套衫	
pyjamas /pə'dʒɑːməz/	*n.*	（一套）睡衣裤	
sandal /'sændl/	*n.*	凉鞋	
sleeve /sliːv/	*n.*	袖子	
sleeveless /'sliːvləs/	*adj.*	无袖的	
stripe /straɪp/	*n.*	条纹；线条	
sweatshirt /'swetʃɜːt/	*n.*	运动衫	

tracksuit /ˈtræksuːt/	n.	运动服；宽松暖和的衣裤
underpants /ˈʌndəpænts/	n.	内裤
underwear /ˈʌndəweə(r)/	n.	内衣
undress /ʌnˈdres/	v.	（给……）脱衣服
wool /wʊl/	n.	绒，毛；绒线，毛线

进阶加油站

◆ 一词多义

trainer	ring
n. 运动鞋	**n.** 戒指
eg. a pair of trainers 一双运动鞋	eg. a wedding ring 结婚戒指
n. 教练员	**v.** 发出铃声
eg. personal trainer 私人教练	eg. I will ring him up. 我会给他打电话的。

jumper	suit
n. 针织套衫	**n.** 套装；西装
eg. woolen jumper 羊毛套衫	eg. a grey suit 一套灰色西装
n. 跳跃者	**v.** 适合；搭配
eg. a long jumper 跳远运动员	eg. Red suits you. 红色很适合你。

◆ 词汇辨析

• wallet, pocket

wallet：**（放钞票、信用卡的）钱包；皮夹子**
eg. *His wallet was stolen.* 他的钱包被偷了。

pocket：**衣袋；口袋**
eg. *I put the key in my pocket.* 我把钥匙放进了口袋里。

• handbag, purse

handbag：**（女士用的）小手提包**
eg. *That handbag suits my dress.* 那个手提包很适合我的连衣裙。

purse：**（尤指女用的）钱包，皮夹子**
eg. *Her purse is stuffed with cards.* 她的钱包里装满了信用卡。

EXERCISE

✓ MATCH

(　) 1. blouse	a. a long narrow line of colour, that is a different colour from the areas next to it
(　) 2. bracelet	b. the process or the job of washing clothes, sheets, etc.
(　) 3. handbag	c. following a style that is popular at a particular time
(　) 4. handkerchief	d. a piece of clothing that covers the body from the waist down and is divided into two parts to cover each leg separately
(　) 5. pyjamas	e. objects such as rings and necklaces that people wear as decoration
(　) 6. stripe	f. a piece of clothing like a shirt, worn by women
(　) 7. sandal	g. a type of light open shoe that is worn in warm weather
(　) 8. underwear	h. a loose jacket and trousers/pants worn in bed
(　) 9. sleeve	i. a piece of jewellery worn around the wrist or arm
(　) 10. trousers	j. a small piece of material or paper that you use for blowing your nose, etc.
(　) 11. jewellery	k. a part of a piece of clothing that covers all or part of your arm
(　) 12. pattern	l. a regular arrangement of lines, shapes, colours, etc. as a design on material, carpets, etc.
(　) 13. laundry	m. to take off your clothes
(　) 14. fashionable	n. a small bag for money, keys, etc., carried especially by women
(　) 15. material	o. cloth used for making clothes, curtains, etc.
(　) 16. undress	p. clothes that you wear under other clothes and next to the skin

☑ *MULTIPLE CHOICES*

(　) 1. Jacob's mom went out, leaving him to *undress*.

　　A. dress up 　　　　　B. take off his clothes 　　C. get dressed

(　) 2. It becomes *fashionable* to eat hot pot in winter.

　　A. modern 　　　　　B. popular 　　　　　C. classy

(　) 3. After putting all the goods in the plastic bag, she *tied* the ends of the bag

　　together.

　　A. loosened 　　　　B. secured 　　　　　C. fastened

(　) 4. He really wants to buy that golden robe embroidered with（绣着）red thread

　　stitched into a *pattern* of flames.

　　A. structure 　　　　B. design 　　　　　C. mode

(　) 5. Most people wear *tracksuits* to relax and to do exercise.

　　A. spacesuits 　　　　B. jogging suits 　　　C. swimsuits

(　) 6. —What *material* is this T-shirt made of?

　　—Cotton.

　　A. cloth used for making clothes

　　B. a design or type of product

　　C. things that are needed in order to do a particular activity

(　) 7. Nurses have to wear a *uniform*.

　　A. a set of clothes made of the same cloth, including a jacket and trousers or a skirt

　　B. the special set of clothes worn by all members of an organization or a group

　　　at work

　　C. a piece of clothing that consists of trousers and a jacket or shirt sewn together

　　　in one piece

(　) 8. His bone hasn't *knitted* together after one month of rest.

　　A. grown 　　　　　B. covered 　　　　　C. coupled

(　) 9. She put a *collar* around the neck of her dog in case it got lost.

　　A. bell 　　　　　　B. band 　　　　　　C. scarf

(　) 10. He prepared a pair of new *trainers* for the coming competition.

　　A. coachs 　　　　　B. sneakers 　　　　　C. instructors

(　) 11. She tried on the new *pullover* but apparently, she was not satisfied with it.

　　A. jumper 　　　　　B. underwear 　　　　　C. shirt

(   ) 12. They are playing an important *match* against the Lakers.

         A. rival   B. balance   C. competition

(   ) 13. Immediately we arrived at the greenhouse, we smelt a heady *perfume* of the roses.

         A. stink   B. taste   C. scent

☑ *FILLING THE BLANKS*

plastic;	fasten;	label;	laundry;	wool;
pocket;	sunglasses;	leather;	necklace;	belt;
fashion;	purse;	buyers;	cotton;	old-fashioned

1. If you always spend more than you earn, you'll need to tighten your _____.

2. Long skirts have come into _____ again.

3. He took out some money from his coat _____.

4. Lucia wore a shinning diamond _____ around her neck.

5. She wore a pair of _____ and set for her vacation in Hawaii.

6. That lady took a coin out of her _____ and gave it to the begging child.

7. Ninety percent of _____ are more interested in cars' safety and reliability than speed and appearance.

8. These shirts are 100% pure _____.

9. She used an elastic band to _____ her long fair hair at the nape of her neck.

10. You can find the washing instructions on the _____.

11. We were too busy, so we had to have the washing done at the _____.

12. This new invention makes it possible that sheep do not have to be sheared—the _____ falls off naturally.

13. The shoes are made of _____, so it wears very well.

14. She has some _____ values and it is impossible to persuade her.

15. Most supermarkets don't provide free _____ bags because these bags can lead to white pollution.

 SPEAKING

Here is the photograph, and it shows friends spending time together. Talk on your own about the photograph for one minute.

 CHECK

1. 耳环 _____

2. 手镯 _____

3. 戒指 _____

4. jacket _____

5. jewellery _____

6. suit _____

7. 围巾 _____

8.（分手指的）手套 _____

9. 领带 _____

10. uniform _____

11. purse _____

12. raincoat _____

13. 项链 _____

14. 品牌 _____

15. 衣领 _____

16. logo _____

17. old-fashioned _____

18. perfume _____

19. 套头毛衣 _____

20. 条纹 _____

Day ⑪ *Shopping* 购物

VOCABULARY

 基础词汇

词 汇	词 义		默写
bill /bɪl/	*n.*	账单	
cash /kæʃ/	*n.*	现金	
change /tʃeɪndʒ/	*n.*	找给的零钱 *v.* 换零钱	
cheap /tʃiːp/	*adj.*	便宜的	
cheque /tʃek/	*n.*	支票	
closed /kləʊzd/	*adj.*	停止营业；关闭	
cost /kɒst/	*n.*	费用；成本	
	v.	需付费；价钱为	
credit card	*n.*	信用卡	
customer /ˈkʌstəmə(r)/	*n.*	顾客	
discount /ˈdɪskaʊnt/	*n.*	折扣	
expensive /ɪkˈspensɪv/	*adj.*	昂贵的	
go shopping		去购物	
pay for		支付	
payment /ˈpeɪmənt/	*n.*	付款	
penny /ˈpeni/	*n.*	便士	
price /praɪs/	*n.*	价格	
half price	*n.*	半价	
receipt /rɪˈsiːt/	*n.*	收据	
rent /rent/	*v.*	租用；租借； *n.* 租金	

sell /sel/	v.	售卖	
shop assistant	n.	店员；售货员	
shopper /ˈʃɒpə(r)/	n.	购物者	
shopping /ˈʃɒpɪŋ/	n.	购物	
shopping mall	n.	购物商场；购物广场	
spend /spend/	v.	花费	
store /stɔː(r)/	n.	商店	
supermarket /ˈsuːpəmɑːkɪt/	n.	超市	
try on		试穿（衣物）	

☑ 重点词汇

词汇	词义		默写
bargain /ˈbɑːgən/	v.	讨价还价；商讨条件	
	n.	协议；交易	
cashpoint /ˈkæʃpɔɪnt/	n.	自动取款机	
complain /kəmˈpleɪn/	v.	抱怨；投诉	
complaint /kəmˈpleɪnt/	n.	抱怨；投诉	
damage /ˈdæmɪdʒ/	v.	损伤；毁坏	
deposit /dɪˈpɒzɪt/	n.	存款	
display /dɪˈspleɪ/	v.	陈列；展出；展示	
exchange /ɪksˈtʃeɪndʒ/	n.	交换；兑换	
hire /ˈhaɪə(r)/	v.	租用；租借	
inexpensive /ˌɪnɪkˈspensɪv/	adj.	不昂贵的	
label /ˈleɪbl/	n.	标签	
logo /ˈləʊgəʊ/	n.	标识；标志	
luxurious /lʌgˈʒʊəriəs/	adj.	十分舒适的；奢侈的	
luxury /ˈlʌkʃəri/	n.	奢侈的享受；奢华；奢侈品	
price tag	n.	价格标签	
quality /ˈkwɒləti/	n.	质量；品质	
quantity /ˈkwɒntəti/	n.	数量	

reasonable /ˈriːznəbl/	adj.	不太贵的；公道的；合理的
reduce /rɪˈdjuːs/	v.	减少；缩小
reduction /rɪˈdʌkʃn/	n.	减价；折扣
refund /ˈriːfʌnd/	n.	退款
retail /ˈriːteɪl/	n.	零售
sale /seɪl/	n.	出售；销售
for sale		待售；供出售
on sale		出售；折价销售
salesman /ˈseɪlzmən/	n.	售货员；推销员
saleswoman /ˈseɪlzwʊmən/	n.	女售货员；女推销员
saving /ˈseɪvɪŋ/	n.	节省；节约
savings /ˈseɪvɪŋz/	n.	存款
second-hand	adj.	旧的；二手的
souvenir /ˌsuːvəˈnɪə(r)/	n.	纪念品；礼物

☑ 进阶加油站

◆ 常用货币单位

中文	英文	缩写	符号
人民币	yuan	RMB	¥
港币	Hong Kong dollar	HKD	HK$
欧元	euro	EUR	€
美元	dollar	USD	$
英镑	pound	GBP	£
加元	Canadian dollar	CAD	C$
澳元	Austrilia dollar	AUD	A$
日元	(Janpanese) yen	JPY	JPY ¥

EXERCISE

MATCH

( ) 1. bill

( ) 2. cash

( ) 3. discount

( ) 4. logo

( ) 5. price

( ) 6. spend

( ) 7. expensive

( ) 8. bargain

( ) 9. complain

( ) 10. exchange

( ) 11. luxurious

( ) 12. price tag

( ) 13. quantity

( ) 14. souvenir

( ) 15. display

( ) 16. reduction

( ) 17. quality

( ) 18. hire

( ) 19. reasonable

( ) 20. retail

a. to give money to pay for goods, services, etc.

b. a label on sth. that shows how much you must pay

c. the standard of sth. when it is compared to other things like it

d. an amount or a number of sth.

e. costing a lot of money

f. a piece of paper that shows how much you owe sb. for goods or services

g. to put sth. in a place where people can see it easily

h. to discuss prices, conditions, etc. with sb in order to reach an agreement that is acceptable

i. the selling of goods to the public, usually through shops

j. an amount of money that is taken off the usual cost of sth.

k. to pay money to borrow sth. for a short time

l. a printed design or symbol that a company or an organization uses as its special sign

m. very comfortable; containing expensive and enjoyable things

n. something that you bring back for other people when you have been on holiday

o. an act of giving sth. to sb. or doing sth. for sb. and receiving sth. in return

p. money in the form of coins or notes/bills

q. not too expensive

r. an amount of money by which sth. is made cheaper

s. to say that you are annoyed, unhappy or not satisfied about sb./sth.

t. the amount of money that you have to pay for sth.

☑ *MULTIPLE CHOICES*

( ) 1. Your kids usually get their good *qualities* by learning from you, so you need to set a good model for them.

    A. minds   B. characteristics   C. abilities

( ) 2. The quality of *customer* service is extremely important for a successful company.

    A. custom   B. costume   C. consumer

( ) 3. Nowadays, most of the businessmen would *spend* enormous amounts advertising their products.

    A. cost   B. invest   C. require

( ) 4. There will be thousands of antiques of the Ming Dynasty *on display* next Monday in the National Museum.

    A. on play   B. on release   C. on show

( ) 5. According to the regulation, all full-time staff can get a 40 percent *discount*.

    A. reduction   B. account   C. count

( ) 6. There are a large variety of good and *inexpensive* restaurants in the town.

    A. cheap   B. dear   C. priceless

( ) 7. With the successful implementation of targeted poverty alleviation policies, it seems *reasonable* to expect rapid rural growth in the coming 20 years.

    A. illogical   B. impossible   C. possible

( ) 8. I think it is necessary to take those boots back and ask for a *refund* since they are not suitable.

    A. payment   B. cheque   C. receipt

( ) 9. There has been some *reduction* in unemployment since the government made a series of employment policies.

    A. increase   B. decrease   C. tension

( ) 10. We are searching for a product that is cheap to produce in large *quantities*.

    A. qualities   B. amounts   C. models

( ) 11. He and his partner had made a *bargain* to tell each other everything.

    A. agreement   B. plan   C. margin

( ) 12. I bought the ring in the street as a *souvenir* of Paris.

    A. representative   B. replacement   C. memento

(　　) 13. The contestants（参赛者）have _hired_ lawyers and are preparing to sue the

organizers.

A. employed　　　　　B. rented　　　　　C. lent

(　　) 14. The tour group _complained about_ the high cost of visiting Japan.

A. praised　　　　　B. were delighted with　　C. felt unsatisfied with

✅ FILLING THE BLANKS

bargained;	**salesman;**	**try on;**	**change;**	**quality;**
refund;	**cost;**	**deposit;**	**cheque;**	**complaints;**
savings;	**retail;**	**rent;**	**display;**	**luxury**

1. Can you help me to _____ a dollar bill for four quarters?

2. Before he left, my father handed me an envelope with a _____ for $2,000.

3. We received many letters of _____ from customers about the lack of charging points.

4. I have bought a new boiler which can make big _____ on fuel bills.

5. Most _____ stores expect to contribute half of their annual profits during the Spring

Festival.

6. Fruit was a _____ in wartime Britain.

7. Many international students work to pay the _____ while they go to college.

8. During the past two years, the _____ of a loaf of bread has increased eight-fold.

9. _____ clothing and shoes to make sure they fit.

10. I _____ with the seller over the price of the painting.

11. When I walked into that building, an insurance _____ walked towards me and tried

to persuade me to buy his product for almost an hour.

12. It is a common sense that when costs are cut product _____ suffers.

13. If there is a delay of 15 hours or more, you will receive a full _____ of the price of

your plane ticket.

14. Steven is rich and he has a large _____ in the bank.

15. The online exhibition recently gives global artists an opportunity to _____ their work.

 **READING**

Questions 1-6

For each question, choose the correct answer.

Organic Food

For me, buying organic is the only way to go. Organic food is more 1 _____ because of high production costs and a lack of widespread 2 _____, but I think there are loads of heath 3 _____.

I prefers purchasing goods produced with 4 _____ benefits. I would buy goods produced naturally despite higher prices, because pesticides and other chemicals create problems 5 _____ for wildlife but also for the plants they're meant to protect.

I also try to buy locally to keep my carbon footprint to a 6 _____, and it's better for the local economy too.

1. A. cheap	B. high	C. expensive	D. low
2. A. goal	B. demand	C. advantage	D. necessity
3. A. benefits	B. damages	C. harm	D. goods
4. A. social	B. environmental	C. economic	D. cultural
5. A. not only	B. only	C. not have	D. only have
6. A. decrease	B. increase	C. maximum	D. minimum

CHECK

1. bill _____ 2. cheque _____ 3. discount _____

4. 顾客 _____ 5. 价格 _____ 6. 租用；租借 _____

7. payment _____ 8. store _____ 9. receipt _____

10. 抱怨；投诉 _____ 11. 讨价还价 _____ 12. 存款 _____

13. quality _____ 14. quantity _____ 15. refund _____

Day ⑫ Personal Feelings, Opinions and Experiences
个人情感、意见与经历

VOCABULARY

✓ 基础词汇

词汇	词义	默写
afraid /əˈfreɪd/	*adj.* 害怕的	
alone /əˈləʊn/	*adj.* 单独的	
amazing /əˈmeɪzɪŋ/	*adj.* 令人大为惊奇的	
angry /ˈæŋgri/	*adj.* 愤怒的	
beautiful /ˈbjuːtɪfl/	*adj.* 美丽的	
better /ˈbetə(r)/	*adj.* 更好的	
bored /bɔːd/	*adj.* （对某人/某物）厌倦的；烦闷的	
boring /ˈbɔːrɪŋ/	*adj.* 没趣的；令人厌倦（或厌烦的）	
brave /breɪv/	*adj.* 勇敢的	
brilliant /ˈbrɪliənt/	*adj.* 聪颖的；很好的	
careful /ˈkeəfl/	*adj.* 仔细的	
clear /klɪə(r)/	*adj.* 清楚的	
clever /ˈklevə(r)/	*adj.* 聪明的	
difficult /ˈdɪfɪkəlt/	*adj.* 困难的	
excellent /ˈeksələnt/	*adj.* 杰出的	
famous /ˈfeɪməs/	*adj.* 著名的	

favourite /ˈfeɪvərɪt/	adj. 特别喜欢的	
free /friː/	adj. 自由的	
friendly /ˈfrendli/	adj. 友好的	
funny /ˈfʌni/	adj. 滑稽的；可笑的	
hungry /ˈhʌŋgri/	adj. 饥饿的；渴望的	
important /ɪmˈpɔːtnt/	adj. 重要的	
kind /kaɪnd/	adj. 友好的	
lovely /ˈlʌvli/	adj. 美丽的；迷人的	
lucky /ˈlʌki/	adj. 幸运的	
modern /ˈmɒdn/	adj. 现代的	
nice /naɪs/	adj. 令人愉快的；友好的	
noisy /ˈnɔɪzi/	adj. 嘈杂的；吵闹的	
pleasant /ˈpleznt/	adj. 令人愉快的	
ready /ˈredi/	adj. 准备好的	
special /ˈspeʃl/	adj. 特殊的	
strange /streɪndʒ/	adj. 奇怪的；陌生的	
strong /strɒŋ/	adj. 坚强的；强壮的	
terrible /ˈterəbl/	adj. 可怕的	
tired /ˈtaɪəd/	adj. 疲倦的	
unhappy /ʌnˈhæpi/	adj. 不快乐的	
useful /ˈjuːsfl/	adj. 有用的	
worried /ˈwʌrid/	adj. 担心的	

✅ 重点词汇

词 汇	词 义	默 写
amusing /əˈmjuːzɪŋ/	adj. 有乐趣的；好笑的	
annoyed /əˈnɔɪd/	adj. 恼怒的	
anxious /ˈæŋkʃəs/	adj. 焦虑的	
ashamed /əˈʃeɪmd/	adj. 惭愧的；羞愧的	

bossy /ˈbɒsi/	*adj.*	专横的
calm /kɑːm/	*adj.*	镇静的；沉着的
challenging /ˈtʃælɪndʒɪŋ/	*adj.*	挑战性的；考验能力的
charming /ˈtʃɑːmɪŋ/	*adj.*	迷人的
cheerful /ˈtʃɪəfl/	*adj.*	令人愉快的
confusing /kənˈfjuːzɪŋ/	*adj.*	难以理解的；不清楚的
cruel /ˈkruːəl/	*adj.*	残酷的；残忍的
curious /ˈkjʊəriəs/	*adj.*	好奇的
delighted /dɪˈlaɪtɪd/	*adj.*	高兴的；愉快的
depressed /dɪˈprest/	*adj.*	沮丧的
enjoyable /ɪnˈdʒɔɪəbl/	*adj.*	令人愉快的
fantastic /fænˈtæstɪk/	*adj.*	极好的
fond /fɒnd/	*adj.*	喜欢的
generous /ˈdʒenərəs/	*adj.*	慷慨的；宽厚的；仁慈的
gentle /ˈdʒentl/	*adj.*	温和的
guilty /ˈgɪlti/	*adj.*	感到内疚的；有罪责的
impressed /ɪmˈprest/	*adj.*	（对……）钦佩，敬仰，有深刻的好印象
intelligent /ɪnˈtelɪdʒənt/	*adj.*	聪明的；有才智的
jealous /ˈdʒeləs/	*adj.*	妒忌的
keen /kiːn/	*adj.*	热情的；热心的
miserable /ˈmɪzrəbl/	*adj.*	痛苦的；非常难受的
negative /ˈnegətɪv/	*adj.*	消极的
nervous /ˈnɜːvəs/	*adj.*	焦虑的
ordinary /ˈɔːdnri/	*adj.*	普通的；平常的；一般的
original /əˈrɪdʒənl/	*adj.*	起初的；最早的
patient /ˈpeɪʃnt/	*adj.*	有耐心的
positive /ˈpɒzətɪv/	*adj.*	积极的
realistic /ˌriːəˈlɪstɪk/	*adj.*	现实的；逼真的
relaxed /rɪˈlækst/	*adj.*	放松的

reliable /rɪˈlaɪəbl/	*adj.*	可信赖的；可靠的
relieved /rɪˈliːvd/	*adj.*	放心的；感到宽慰的
rude /ruːd/	*adj.*	粗鲁的
serious /ˈsɪəriəs/	*adj.*	严重的；严肃的；认真的
slim /slɪm/	*adj.*	苗条的
smart /smɑːt/	*adj.*	聪明的
stupid /ˈstjuːpɪd/	*adj.*	愚蠢的
typical /ˈtɪpɪkl/	*adj.*	典型的；一贯的；平常的

✅ 进阶加油站

◆ 词汇辨析

- interested, interesting

  interested：**感兴趣的**

  interesting：**有趣的；有吸引力的**

  eg. *I am interested in reading.* 我很喜欢看书。

  　　This novel is interesting. 这本小说很有趣。

- confused, confusing

  confused：**迷惑的；难懂的**

  confusing：**难以理解的；不清楚的**

  eg. *I am confused about this question.* 我对这个问题感到很困惑。

  　　This question is confusing. 这个问题令人费解。

- disappointed, disappointing

  disappointed：**失望的；沮丧的**

  disappointing：**令人失望的；令人沮丧的**

  eg. *The coach was disappointed with the result of the match.* 教练对比赛结果很失望。

  　　The result of the match is disappointing. 比赛结果令人失望。

- embarrassed, embarrassing

  embarrassed：**尴尬的；害羞的**

  embarrassing：**使人尴尬的；使人害羞的**

eg. *I always feel embarrassed when I am on the stage.*

当我站在舞台上时，我总是感到很尴尬。

That is an embarrassing situation. 那是一个令人尴尬的处境。

- excited, exciting

excited：**激动的；兴奋的**

exciting：**令人激动的；使人兴奋的**

eg. *The students were excited about the school trip.* 学生们对学校旅行很兴奋。

It was one of the most exciting moments in my childhood.

这是我童年生活中最激动人心的时刻之一。

- frightened, frightening

frightened：**惊吓的；受惊的；害怕的**

frightening：**引起恐惧的；使惊恐的**

eg. *I am frightened of riding a roller coaster.* 我害怕坐过山车。

It's such a frightening experience. 这是一个很可怕的经历。

- satisfied, satisfying

satisfied：**满意的；满足的**

satisfying：**令人满意的；令人满足的**

eg. *The team members are not satisfied with the result.* 队员们对这个结果不满意。

It's satisfying to watch a movie at home on rainy day.

下雨天在家里看电影是一件惬意的事。

- bored, boring

bored：**对（某人 / 某物）厌倦的；烦闷的**

boring：**没趣的；令人厌倦（或厌烦）的**

eg. *Students got bored with his speech.* 学生们厌倦了他的演讲。

His speech is boring. 他的演讲很无聊。

- amazed, amazing

amazed：**大为惊奇的**

amazing：**令人大为惊奇的**

eg. *Colleagues were amazed at his success.* 他的成功使同事们大为惊奇。

This is an amazing success. 这是一个惊人的成功。

 **EXERCISE**

✅ MATCH

( ) 1. brave	a. anxious about sth. or afraid of sth.
( ) 2. special	b. funny and enjoyable
( ) 3. useful	c. upset because sth. you hoped for has not happened
( ) 4. famous	d. having or showing a lack of respect for other people and their feelings
( ) 5. alone	e. without any other people
( ) 6. careful	f. having great power
( ) 7. nervous	g. that can help you to do or achieve what you want
( ) 8. strong	h. pleased because you have achieved sth.
( ) 9. relaxed	i. known about by many people
( ) 10. guilty	j. unable to think clearly
( ) 11. amusing	k. giving a lot of attention to details
( ) 12. bossy	l. having a strong desire to know about sth.
( ) 13. patient	m. willing to do things which are difficult, dangerous or painful
( ) 14. curious	n. able to wait for a long time or accept annoying behaviour or difficulties without becoming angry
( ) 15. disappointed	o. that can be trusted to do sth. well
( ) 16. negative	p. calm and not anxious or worried
( ) 17. rude	q. not ordinary or usual
( ) 18. reliable	r. considering only the bad side of sth./sb.
( ) 19. satisfied	s. always telling people what to do
( ) 20. confused	t. feeling ashamed because you have done sth. that you know is wrong

☑ *MULTIPLE CHOICES*

(   ) 1. The statement is so *confusing* that nobody knows what the president wants to do.

      A. amazing   B. puzzling   C. mixing

(   ) 2. When she went for a walk in the park, she saw many *strange* faces in the crowd.

      A. unknown   B. dangerous   C. special

(   ) 3. I often have *terrible* nightmares, so I always sleep with the light on.

      A. worried   B. bored   C. horrible

(   ) 4. I felt incredibly *ashamed* of myself for getting so angry for such a trifling（微不足道的）thing.

      A. proud   B. pleasant   C. embarrassed

(   ) 5. The kid is so lonely and *hungry* for love.

      A. satisfied   B. desired   C. impatient

(   ) 6. She is *annoyed* that her family won't allow her to work with children.

      A. angry   B. pleasant   C. guilty

(   ) 7. We felt at home with her and *were impressed* with the depth of her knowledge.

      A. felt angry   B. felt admiration   C. felt confident

(   ) 8. She was *jealous of* his success and possessions after divorce, so she planned a revenge towards him.

      A. green-eyed   B. red-eyed   C. yellow-eyed

(   ) 9. Bella is a very *intelligent* woman who knows her own mind.

      A. smart   B. modern   C. thoughtful

(   ) 10. Jack took a series of badly paid secretarial jobs after graduation which made him really *miserable*.

      A. poor   B. difficult   C. unhappy

(   ) 11. William was always *generous* in sharing his enormous knowledge.

      A. mean   B. adequate   C. friendly

(   ) 12. She was *frightened* of making a mistake, so she checked her paper again and again before handing in.

      A. afraid   B. bored   C. confused

(   ) 13. Michael was *serious* about making a proposal to his girlfriend.

A. worried   B. sincere   C. careless

(   ) 14. The five-year-old boy's knowledge was *out of the ordinary*.

A. common   B. general   C. unusual

(   ) 15. Our boss took us to a *fantastically* expensive restaurant which was amazing!

A. wonderfully   B. extremely   C. excellently

☑ *FILLING THE BLANKS*

reliable;	patiently;	embarrassing;	guilty;	afraid;
depressed;	relieved;	cruelly;	original;	modern;
slim;	noisily;	typical;	realistic;	stupid

1. Cinderella was often _____ tormented（折磨）by her jealous siblings.

2. It is _____ of her to forget so you have to always remind her of those important things.

3. When I was a little child, I thought it was so _____ to sing in public that I avoided taking part in chorus.

4. After the outbreak of the pandemic, you should feel _____ that your job is still safe.

5. All of the visitors are amazed by that extraordinarily _____ painting of Indians.

6. Cherry has been very _____ about the result of the competition.

7. The _____ manuscript has been lost during the World War II, and what you see now is just a copy.

8. Our information comes from a _____ source, so you should just follow our instruction.

9. Forgetting to bring a pen for my final exam made me look _____ .

10. Although there were many people waiting in line, she still sat _____ waiting for her turn to do a small surgery.

11. I used to be _____ of walking home alone in the dark, so I usually stayed at home at night.

12. The accuser claimed the judge had been _____ of a 'gross error of judgment'.

13. This is the most _____ and well-equipped hospital in London, and you can get

the best treatment here.

14. In the P.E. class, you can always find the students on the grass bank cheered _____.

15. I am always asked how to manage to stay so _____ and healthy.

 **LISTENING**

Questions 1-4

For each question, choose the correct answer.

1. You will hear two friends talking about a film.

   How did they react to the ending?

   A. unclear

   B. frightening

   C. surprising

   扫码听录音

2. You will hear two friends talking about an exhibition.

   Why was the woman disappointed with it?

   A. There weren't many paintings.

   B. It was very expensive.

   C. The gallery was too dark.

3. You will hear two friends talking about a tennis match.

   How do they feel?

   A. disappointed at the team's performance

   B. surprised at the result

   C. worried about their future

4. You will hear two friends discussing an article about air pollution.

   The woman is _____.

   A. surprised by some new information

   B. annoyed by the writer's attitude

   C. confused by all the details

CHECK

1. afraid _____

2. boring _____

3. famous _____

4. 愤怒的 _____

5. 勇敢的 _____

6. 杰出的 _____

7. modern _____

8. special _____

9. terrible _____

10. 焦虑的 _____

11. 迷人的 _____

12. 镇静的 _____

13. depressed _____

14. nervous _____

15. enjoyable _____

16. 尴尬的 _____

17. 放松的 _____

18. 愚蠢的 _____

19. ordinary _____

20. positive _____

Day ⑬ Work and Jobs 工作与职业

VOCABULARY

✅ 基础词汇

词 汇	词 义		默 写
actor /ˈæktə(r)/	n.	演员	
artist /ˈɑːtɪst/	n.	艺术家	
boss /bɒs/	n.	老板	
businessman /ˈbɪznəsmæn/	n.	商人	
businesswoman /ˈbɪznəswʊmən/	n.	女商人	
chemist /ˈkemɪst/	n.	化学家	
chef /ʃef/	n.	厨师	
cleaner /ˈkliːnə(r)/	n.	清洁工	
cook /kʊk/	n.	厨师	
dentist /ˈdentɪst/	n.	牙科医生	
drugstore /ˈdrʌgstɔː(r)/	n.	药房	
doctor /ˈdɒktə(r)/	n.	医生	
engineer /ˌendʒɪˈnɪə(r)/	n.	工程师	
explorer /ɪkˈsplɔːrə(r)/	n.	探险者	
farmer /ˈfɑːmə(r)/	n.	农民	
guest /gest/	n.	客人；旅客；旅客；房客	
journalist /ˈdʒɜːnəlɪst/	n.	新闻工作者	
manager /ˈmænɪdʒə(r)/	n.	经理	

mechanic /məˈkænɪk/	n.	技工
meeting /ˈmiːtɪŋ/	n.	会议
nurse /nɜːs/	n.	护士
occupation /ˌɒkjuˈpeɪʃn/	n.	工作；职业
painter /ˈpeɪntə(r)/	n.	画家
photographer /fəˈtɒgrəfə(r)/	n.	摄影师
police officer	n.	警察
receptionist /rɪˈsepʃənɪst/	n.	接待员
secretary /ˈsekrətri/	n.	秘书
shop assistant	n.	售货员
staff /stɑːf/	n.	全体职工
tennis player	n.	网球运动员
worker /ˈwɜːkə(r)/	n.	工人

✅ 重点词汇

词 汇	词 义	默 写
architect /ˈɑːkɪtekt/	n. 建筑师	
army /ˈɑːmi/	n. 军队	
application /ˌæplɪˈkeɪʃn/	n. 申请	
astronaut /ˈæstrənɔːt/	n. 宇航员	
athlete /ˈæθliːt/	n. 运动员	
babysitter /ˈbeɪbisɪtə(r)/	n. 临时保姆	
banker /ˈbæŋkə(r)/	n. 银行家	
barber /ˈbɑːbə(r)/	n. 理发师	
butcher /ˈbʊtʃə(r)/	n. 屠夫	
cameraman /ˈkæmrəmæn/	n. 摄影师；摄像师	
candidate /ˈkændɪdət/	n. 候选人；申请人；应试者	
captain /ˈkæptɪn/	n. 船长	
conference /ˈkɒnfərəns/	n. 会议	

contract /ˈkɒntrækt/	*n.*	合同
crew /kruː/	*n.*	（轮船、飞机等上面的）全体工作人员
customs officer	*n.*	海关官员
designer /dɪˈzaɪnə(r)/	*n.*	设计师
detective /dɪˈtektɪv/	*n.*	侦探
director /dəˈrektə(r)/	*n.*	经理；导演；主管
diver /ˈdaɪvə(r)/	*n.*	潜水员
earn /ɜːn/	*v.*	挣得；赚得；赢得
employee /ɪmˈplɔiiː/	*n.*	雇员
employer /ɪmˈplɔiə(r)/	*n.*	雇主
employment /ɪmˈplɔimənt/	*n.*	工作；职业；就业
firefighter /ˈfaɪəfaɪtə(r)/	*n.*	消防队员
goalkeeper /ˈɡəʊlkiːpə(r)/	*n.*	守门员
guard /ɡɑːd/	*n.*	警卫
hairdresser /ˈheədresə(r)/	*n.*	理发师
instruction /ɪnˈstrʌkʃn/	*n.*	用法说明；操作指南
judge /dʒʌdʒ/	*n.*	法官
lawyer /ˈlɔːjə(r)/	*n.*	律师
lecturer /ˈlektʃərə(r)/	*n.*	讲师
librarian /laɪˈbreəriən/	*n.*	图书管理员
model /ˈmɒdl/	*n.*	模特儿
novelist /ˈnɒvəlɪst/	*n.*	小说家
pilot /ˈpaɪlət/	*n.*	飞行员；（航空器）驾驶员
poet /ˈpəʊɪt/	*n.*	诗人
porter /ˈpɔːtə(r)/	*n.*	行李员；搬运工
postman /ˈpəʊstmən/	*n.*	邮递员
president /ˈprezɪdənt/	*n.*	总统
profession /prəˈfeʃn/	*n.*	职业
professional /prəˈfeʃnl/	*adj.*	专业的；职业的
professor /prəˈfesə(r)/	*n.*	教授

programmer /ˈprəʊgræmə(r)/	n.	程序设计员；编程人员
publisher /ˈpʌblɪʃə(r)/	n.	出版人（或机构）
qualification /ˌkwɒlɪfɪˈkeɪʃn/	n.	资格
quit /kwɪt/	v.	离开；离任；离校
reporter /rɪˈpɔːtə(r)/	n.	记者
retire /rɪˈtaɪə(r)/	v.	（使）退休
retirement /rɪˈtaɪəmənt/	n.	退休
sailor /ˈseɪlə(r)/	n.	水手
salary /ˈsæləri/	n.	薪水（尤指按月发放的）
sales assistant	n.	销售助理
salesman /ˈseɪlzmən/	n.	推销员
saleswoman /ˈseɪlzwʊmən/	n.	女售货员
scientist /ˈsaɪəntɪst/	n.	科学家
security guard	n.	保安人员
soldier /ˈsəʊldʒə(r)/	n.	士兵
unemployed /ˌʌnɪmˈplɔɪd/	adj.	失业的
volunteer /ˌvɒlənˈtɪə(r)/	n.	志愿者
wage /weɪdʒ/	n.	（通常指按周领的）工资

✅ 进阶加油站

◆ 词汇辨析

work, job, career

work 是对工作的泛指，可以指工作或者劳动，不可数名词。

eg. *There is plenty of work to be done in the factory.* 工厂里还有很多工作需要做。

job 是指谋生的、可以领取薪水的具体的工作，可数名词。

eg. *He took a job as a waiter.* 他找了一个当服务员的工作。

career 是指个人的职业生涯，需要付出心血和精力，可以包括多年来从事的许多不同的工作。

eg. *She started her career as a dancer.* 她开启了舞者的职业生涯。

EXERCISE

✓ MATCH

( ) 1. architect

( ) 2. conference

( ) 3. astronaut

( ) 4. president

( ) 5. babysitter

( ) 6. postman

( ) 7. cameraman

( ) 8. cook

( ) 9. mechanic

( ) 10. volunteer

( ) 11. earn

( ) 12. receptionist

( ) 13. designer

( ) 14. porter

( ) 15. professor

( ) 16. barber

( ) 17. firefighter

( ) 18. army

a. a person whose job is repairing machines, especially the engines of vehicles

b. a person who does a job without being paid for it

c. a person whose job is to decide how things such as clothes, furniture, tools, etc. will look or work by making drawings, plans or patterns

d. the leader of a republic, especially the US

e. a person whose job is to deal with people arriving at or telephoning a hotel, an office building, a doctor's surgery, etc.

f. a university teacher of the highest rank

g. a person who takes care of babies or children while their parents are away from home and is usually paid to do this

h. a person whose job is designing buildings, etc.

i. a person whose job is to put out fires

j. a large organized group of soldiers who are trained to fight on land

k. a person whose job involves travelling and working in a spacecraft

l. a person whose job is to cut men's hair and sometimes to shave them

m. a person whose job is operating a camera for making films or television programmes

n. a person who cooks food or whose job is cooking

o. a person whose job is carrying people's bags and other loads

p. a meeting at which people have formal discussions

q. to get money for work that you do

r. a person whose job is to collect and deliver letters, etc

✓ *MULTIPLE CHOICES*

(   ) 1. Sam is the perfect *candidate* for the job.

     A. person being considered   B. person being eliminated   C. person being chosen

(   ) 2. Juliana finds a new job recently with a weekly *wage* of 200 dollars.

     A. money that employees earn for doing their job, usually paid every month

     B. money that employees get for doing their job, usually paid every week

     C. money that you spend on sth.

(   ) 3. Ivy was forced to *retire* early from teaching because of her poor body condition.

     A. stop doing her job

     B. continue to do her job

     C. delay retirement

(   ) 4. 'If I don't get more money I'll *quit*,' he said to his boss angrily.

     A. sue you   B. blame you   C. leave my job

(   ) 5. We have made an appointment with the supplier to sign *a contract* next Monday morning.

     A. an informal oral agreement

     B. a formal oral agreement

     C. an official written agreement

(   ) 6. Please state your name, age and *occupation* below.

     A. job   B. hobby   C. address

(   ) 7. She couldn't find any regular *employment*.

     A. salary   B. job   C. task

(   ) 8. He is *an employee* of clothing factory, which is paid weekly.

     A. a board officer   B. a worker   C. a boss

(   ) 9. The *judge* adjourned (暂停) the hearing until next month.

     A. justice   B. referee   C. lawyer

(   ) 10. To be a successful *novelist*, you must have absolute belief in your story.

     A. poet   B. director   C. fictionist

(   ) 11. You can obtain the medicine from all the available *pharmacy*.

     A. grocery store   B. drugstore   C. hospital

( ) 12. He spends twenty years as an airline *pilot*, and all of his customers are satisfied with his service.

A. person in charge of an aircraft

B. person in charge of a ship

C. a person in charge of an orchestra

( ) 13. Before assembling your computer, I suggest you to look at the *instructions*.

A. conductors   B. commanders   C. directions

( ) 14. Vivian has recently found a job to be *a lecturer* in law.

A. a teacher of the highest rank

B. an associate professor

C. a teacher at a university or college

☑ *FILLING THE BLANKS*

professional;	salary;	staff;	earn;	director;
unemployed;	dentist;	retirement;	guests;	guards;
captain;	journalist;	detective;	athlete;	secretary

1. If a company wants to be successful, it must _____ the reputation for honesty.

2. If the tooth feels very loose, the _____ may recommend you to pull it out.

3. The hotel can accommodate for 500 _____.

4. I am a little busy now. You can call my _____ to make an appointment.

5. She is good at all kinds of sports. I believe she must be a natural _____.

6. The _____ gave the order to abandon ship before the ship almost sank.

7. Now the _____ Arthur Conan Doyle is appealing for witnesses who may have seen anything suspicious last night.

8. According to a recent report, the proportion of those who are over _____ age has grown tremendously in the past ten years.

9. The lawyer was paid a huge _____ for his winning of an important law suit.

10. The government wanted to create jobs for the _____.

11. The prisoners overpowered their _____ and ran out of the jail.

12. Some parents got contact with the _____ of education to complain about the heavy burden of their children.

13. My job as a _____ is to make objective reporting and expose truths to the public.

14. The emergency department of the hospital has a _____ of five people, and you can ask help from any of them.

15. That art student used to play _____ football for a short time.

✓ READING

Questions 1-6

For each question, choose the correct answer.

Dear Sir/Madam,

I saw your advertisement on the website and I am interested in the 1 _____ for marketing manager in your hotel. I attach my resume and an 2 _____ form in this email.

I have several professional 3 _____ and I have just finished a training course at the local college in marketing. I have a great passion in having a 4 _____ in the hotel business, and I have worked in this industry for 7 years.

I have good communication 5 _____ and I am also reliable, 6 _____ and enthusiastic. I can provide you with excellent reference from my previous employers.

Looking forward to your reply.

Yours sincerely,
Elena

1. A. vacant	B. vacancy	C. career	D. profession
2. A. application	B. apply	C. register	D. registration
3. A. references	B. advantages	C. qualifications	D. demonstrations
4. A. work	B. career	C. employment	D. employer
5. A. goods	B. skills	C. opportunities	D. interests
6. A. effect	B. affect	C. effective	D. efficient

CHECK

1. dentist _____

2. engineer _____

3. goalkeeper_____

4. 飞行员 _____

5. 经理 _____

6. 宇航员 _____

7. athlete _____

8. conference _____

9. designer _____

10. 诗人 _____

11. 候选人 _____

12. 侦探 _____

13. wage _____

14. salesman _____

15. sailor _____

16. 资格 _____

17. 程序设计员 _____

18. 教授 _____

19. retirement _____

20. soldier _____

Day 14 *Travel and Transport*

旅行与交通

 VOCABULARY

☑ 基础词汇

词汇	词义		默写
airport /ˈeəpɔːt/	n.	机场	
ambulance /ˈæmbjələns/	n.	救护车	
backpack /ˈbækpæk/	n.	背包；旅行包	
coach /kəʊtʃ/	n.	教练；长途汽车	
country /ˈkʌntri/	n.	国家	
delay /dɪˈleɪ/	v.	延迟；延期	
flight /flaɪt/	n.	航班	
guidebook /ˈgaɪdbʊk/	n.	旅游指南（或手册）	
helicopter /ˈhelɪkɒptə(r)/	n.	直升机	
journey /ˈdʒɜːni/	n.	（尤指长途）旅行	
luggage /ˈlʌgɪdʒ/	n.	行李	
motorbike /ˈməʊtəbaɪk/	n.	摩托车	
motorway /ˈməʊtəweɪ/	n.	高速公路	
nationality /ˌnæʃəˈnæləti/	n.	国籍	
passenger /ˈpæsɪndʒə(r)/	n.	乘客	
passport /ˈpɑːspɔːt/	n.	护照	
pilot /ˈpaɪlət/	n.	飞行员	
platform /ˈplætfɔːm/	n.	站台	
railway /ˈreɪlweɪ/	n.	铁路	

reception /rɪˈsepʃn/	n.	接待
suitcase /ˈsuːtkeɪs/	n.	手提箱
taxi /ˈtæksi/	n.	出租汽车
tour guide	n.	导游
tourist /ˈtʊərɪst/	n.	游客
traffic /ˈtræfɪk/	n.	交通
tram /træm/	n.	有轨电车
travel /ˈtrævl/	v.	长途行走；旅行；游历
trip /trɪp/	n.	（尤指短程往返的）旅行，出行
underground /ˌʌndəˈɡraʊnd/	n.	地铁
wheel /wiːl/	n.	车轮；轮子；方向盘

☑ 重点词汇

词 汇	词 义		默 写
abroad /əˈbrɔːd/	adv.	在国外	
accommodation /əˌkɒməˈdeɪʃn/	n.	住宿	
announcement /əˈnaʊnsmənt/	n.	公告；通告	
arrival /əˈraɪvl/	n.	到达	
astronaut /ˈæstrənɔːt/	n.	宇航员	
baggage /ˈbæɡɪdʒ/	n.	行李	
boarding pass	n.	登机牌	
border /ˈbɔːdə(r)/	n.	国界；边界	
brochure /ˈbrəʊʃə(r)/	n.	资料（或广告）手册	
canal /kəˈnæl/	n.	运河	
currency /ˈkʌrənsi/	n.	货币；通货	
Customs /ˈkʌstəmz/	n.	海关	
departure /dɪˈpɑːtʃə(r)/	n.	离开	
destination /ˌdestɪˈneɪʃn/	n.	目的地	
duty-free /ˌdjuːti ˈfriː/	adj.	免关税的	
embassy /ˈembəsi/	n.	大使馆	

exchange rate	*n.*	汇率
fare /feə(r)/	*n.*	车费；船费；飞机票价
ferry /ˈferi/	*n.*	渡船
handlebar /ˈhændlbɑː(r)/	*n.*	（自行车或摩托车的）把手
harbour /ˈhɑːbə(r)/	*n.*	港湾
hitchhike /ˈhɪtʃhaɪk/	*v.*	免费搭便车
immigration /ˌɪmɪˈɡreɪʃn/	*n.*	移民
jet /dʒet/	*n.*	喷气式飞机
reservation /ˌrezəˈveɪʃn/	*n.*	预订
reserve /rɪˈzɜːv/	*v.*	预订；预约
rocket /ˈrɒkɪt/	*n.*	火箭
route /ruːt/	*n.*	路线；常规路线
scooter /ˈskuːtə(r)/	*n.*	小型摩托车
spaceship /ˈspeɪsʃɪp/	*n.*	（航天）飞船
tunnel /ˈtʌnl/	*n.*	隧道
visa /ˈviːzə/	*n.*	签证

✅ 进阶加油站

◆ 高频短语

- **make a reservation** 预订
- **on board** 在船（或飞机、火车）上
- **get/collect your luggage** 取你的行李

◆ 词汇辨析

trip, journey, travel

trip 通常指短程往返的旅行。

eg. *We will have a day trip in the mountains next weekend.* 下个周末我们要去山里一日游。

journey 尤指长途旅行，通常为单程旅行。

eg. *They are going on a journey to Europe.* 他们正在欧洲旅行。

travel 泛指旅行这一行为，通常指长途旅行。

eg. *Do you have any travel plans this year?* 今年你有旅行计划吗?

EXERCISE

✓ MATCH

( ) 1. astronaut

( ) 2. brochure

( ) 3. hitchhike

( ) 4. luggage

( ) 5. guidebook

( ) 6. tourist

( ) 7. announcement

( ) 8. reservation

( ) 9. immigration

( ) 10. harbour

( ) 11. currency

( ) 12. departure

( ) 13. traffic

( ) 14. passenger

( ) 15. journey

( ) 16. motorbike

( ) 17. flight

( ) 18. ambulance

( ) 19. pilot

( ) 20. railway

a. to travel by getting rides from passing vehicles without paying

b. an arrangement for a seat on a plane or train, a room in a hotel, etc. to be kept for you

c. an area of water on the coast, protected from the open sea by strong walls, where ships can shelter

d. the act of leaving a place

e. bags, cases, etc. that contain your clothes and things when you are travelling

f. a bicycle which has a small engine

g. a book that gives information about a place for travellers or tourists

h. a person who operates the controls of an aircraft, especially as a job

i. the system of money that a country uses

j. a track with rails on which trains run

k. a person who is travelling in a car, bus, train, plane or ship and who is not driving it or working on it

l. a person whose job involves travelling and working in a spacecraft

m. an act of travelling from one place to another, especially when they are far apart

n. a journey made by air, especially in a plane

o. a small magazine or book containing pictures and information about sth.

p. a vehicle with special equipment, used for taking sick or injured people to a hospital

q. the vehicles that are on a road at a particular time

r. a person who is travelling or visiting a place for pleasure

s. the process of coming to live permanently in a country that is not your own

t. a spoken or written statement that informs people about sth.

✅ *MULTIPLE CHOICES*

(   ) 1. I'll call the restaurant and make a *reservation*.

       A. arrangement   B. book   C. booking

(   ) 2. We bought lots of *duty-free goods* at the airport.

       A. out of responsibility goods

       B. goods without paying tax

       C. goods without paying money

(   ) 3. The sudden *departure* of the chief manager threw the office into chaos.

       A. death   B. appearance   C. leaving

(   ) 4. After you go through immigration control, you can collect your *baggage*.

       A. luggage   B. passage   C. parcel

(   ) 5. Last Friday morning, the government made *an announcement* about changes to keep economy stable.

       A. a forecast   B. an indication   C. a statement

(   ) 6. The government will provide *temporary accommodation* for up to ten thousand homeless people in the city.

       A. permanent residence   B. shelters   C. large houses

(   ) 7. They are planning a *journey* to Europe.

       A. tour   B. training   C. hiking

(   ) 8. All applicants can take part in the interview regardless of age, sex, religion or *nationality*.

       A. the fact of belonging to a particular race

       B. the legal right of belonging to a particular nation

       C. the language that you learn to speak first as a child

(   ) 9. Cobber used to be the women's football *coach* at the university.

       A. trainee   B. team member   C. trainer

(   ) 10. I will *reserve* a double room with a balcony.

       A. rent   B. buy   C. book

(   ) 11. Please remember to leave your room keys at *reception* when you check out.

       A. front desk

B. informal party

C. office that books rooms for people

(   ) 12. The Sichuan-Tibet Railway will cross eight mountains, and more than 93 percent of the line will consist of bridges and *tunnels*.

A. passages built underground which allow the railway to go through the mountains

B. passages that water can flow along

C. large holes in the side of the mountains

(   ) 13. I always travel by *underground* every day.

A. bus   B. taxi   C. subway

(   ) 14. When you find somebody slip into a coma (昏迷), you'd better call *an ambulance* quickly.

A. a vehicle for patients

B. a rescue worker

C. a professional doctor

☑ FILLING THE BLANKS

border;	immigration;	passport;	delayed;	wheel;
route;	abroad;	spaceship;	platform;	Customs;
traffic;	passenger;	hitchhiked;	motorway;	currency

1. You should take your _____ with you when changing money abroad.

2. The holding of the Beijing 2022 Winter Olympics on schedule is in itself quite a feat, made possible thanks to China largely controlling the virus. The Tokyo 2020 Olympics was _____ for a year.

3. They were stuck in _____ for almost 2 hours and missed their flight.

4. A right-mile stretch of _____ has been closed temporarily due to the thick fog.

5. Mr. Clerk was a _____ on the plane when it crashed.

6. The train now standing at _____ 3 is for Beijing.

7. The _____ have seized large quantities of smuggled goods last Friday.

8. The government has decided to tighten its _____ policies and set higher standards

for those who want to apply for green cards.

9. Neff's car broke down on the half way, so he _____ to New York during his Christmas holiday.

10. Chinese internet search giant Baidu Inc on Wednesday unveiled its first level 5 self-driving robocar with no steering _____.

11. The Centre Avenue is the most direct _____ to the centre of town.

12. I would love to go _____ this year, perhaps to the South of America.

13. Recently, some citizens claimed they have witnessed an alien _____ and posted some related pictures on Facebook.

14. Tourism is the country's top earner of foreign _____.

15. To date, he has managed to identify more than 3,800 plant species in Zhuxi, on the _____ of Shaanxi province and Chongqing municipality.

 SPEAKING

> 1. Do you often cycle to different places? (Why / Why not?)
> 2. How do you prefer to travel on long journeys, car or bus? (Why)

 # CHECK

1. airport _____ 　　2. flight _____ 　　3. helicopter _____

4. 救护车 _____ 　　5. 乘客 _____ 　　6. 护照 _____

7. railway _____ 　　8. backpack _____ 　　9. underground _____

10. 国籍 _____ 　　11. 游客 _____ 　　12. 手提箱 _____

13. accommodation _____ 　　14. border _____ 　　15. departure _____

16. 免关税的 _____ 　　17. 签证 _____ 　　18. 移民 _____

19. embassy _____ 　　20. fare _____

Day 15 The Natural World

自然世界

 VOCABULARY

✅ 基础词汇

词 汇		词 义	默写
air /eə(r)/	n.	空气	
autumn /ˈɔːtəm/	n.	秋天	
bank /bæŋk/	n.	河岸	
beach /biːtʃ/	n.	海滩	
countryside /ˈkʌntrisaɪd/	n.	乡村	
desert /ˈdezət/	n.	沙漠	
field /fiːld/	n.	田；地	
fire /ˈfaɪə(r)/	n.	火	
forest /ˈfɒrɪst/	n.	森林	
grass /grɑːs/	n.	草；草地	
grow /grəʊ/	v.	（使）生长，发育	
hill /hɪl/	n.	小山	
hot /hɒt/	adj.	热的	
ice /aɪs/	n.	冰	
island /ˈaɪlənd/	n.	岛	
lake /leɪk/	n.	湖泊	
moon /muːn/	n.	月亮	
mountain /ˈmaʊntən/	n.	高山	
plant /plɑːnt/	n.	植物	

river /ˈrɪvə(r)/	n.	河；江	
sea /siː/	n.	海；海洋	
sky /skaɪ/	n.	天空	
space /speɪs/	n.	太空；空间	
spring /sprɪŋ/	n.	春天	
star /stɑː(r)/	n.	星星	
summer /ˈsʌmə(r)/	n.	夏天	
winter /ˈwɪntə(r)/	n.	冬天	
wood /wʊd/	n.	树林；木头	
wool /wʊl/	n.	绒，毛；绒线，毛线	
world /wɜːld/	n.	世界	

✓ 重点词汇

词汇	词义		默写
blow /bləʊ/	v.	吹；刮	
branch /brɑːntʃ/	n.	树枝	
breeze /briːz/	n.	微风	
bush /bʊʃ/	n.	灌木	
cave /keɪv/	n.	洞穴	
centigrade /ˈsentɪɡreɪd/	adj.	摄氏的	
cliff /klɪf/	n.	悬崖	
climate /ˈklaɪmət/	n.	气候	
coast /kəʊst/	n.	海岸；海滨	
continent /ˈkɒntɪnənt/	n.	大陆	
degree /dɪˈɡriː/	n.	度；度数	
farmland /ˈfɑːmlænd/	n.	农田	
forecast /ˈfɔːkɑːst/	n./v.	预测	

freeze /friːz/	*v.*	（使）冻结，结冰
gale /geɪl/	*n.*	大风
humid /ˈhjuːmɪd/	*adj.*	温暖潮湿的
jungle /ˈdʒʌŋɡl/	*n.*	（热带）丛林，密林
mild /maɪld/	*adj.*	温和的
planet /ˈplænɪt/	*n.*	行星
rainforest /ˈreɪnfɒrɪst/	*n.*	雨林
range /reɪndʒ/	*n.*	范围；山脉
scenery /ˈsiːnəri/	*n.*	风景
stone /stəʊn/	*n.*	石头
stream /striːm/	*n.*	小河；溪
sunrise /ˈsʌnraɪz/	*n.*	日出
sunset /ˈsʌnset/	*n.*	日落
valley /ˈvæli/	*n.*	山谷
waterfall /ˈwɔːtəfɔːl/	*n.*	瀑布
wave /weɪv/	*n.*	波浪

✅ 进阶加油站

◆ 方位词大总结

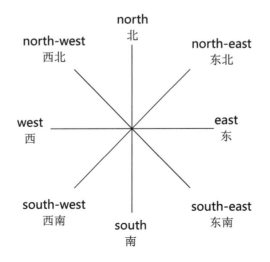

113

◆ 天气词汇大总结

sun	*n.* 太阳	sunny	*adj.* 晴朗的
cloud	*n.* 云	cloudy	*adj.* 多云的；阴天的
rain	*n.* 雨	rainy	*adj.* 阴雨的；多雨的
snow	*n.* 雪	snowy	*adj.* 下雪的
storm	*n.* 暴风雨	stormy	*adj.* 有暴风雨（或暴风雪）的
fog	*n.* 雾	foggy	*adj.* 有雾的
wind	*n.* 风	windy	*adj.* 多风的；风大的
ice	*n.* 冰	icy	*adj.* 冰冷的；冰冻的
breeze	*n.* 微风	breezy	*adj.* 有微风的
lightning	*n.* 闪电	thunder	*n.* 雷；雷声
haze	*n.* 雾霭；薄雾	sandstorm	*n.* 沙暴
typhoon	*n.* 台风	blizzard	*n.* 暴风雪；雪暴
shower	*n.* 阵雨；阵雪	mist	*n.* 薄雾；水汽
flood	*n.* 洪水；水灾	drought	*n.* 久旱；旱灾

EXERCISE

✓ MATCH

( ) 1. valley	a. an extremely strong wind
( ) 2. waterfall	b. a thick forest in tropical parts of the world that have a lot of rain
( ) 3. jungle	c. a statement about what will happen in the future, based on information that is available now
( ) 4. gale	d. (of the air or climate) warm and damp
( ) 5. continent	e. a large hole in the side of a hill or under the ground
( ) 6. rainforest	f. the regular pattern of weather conditions of a particular place
( ) 7. cave	g. the land beside or near to the sea or ocean
( ) 8. thunder	h. land that is used for farming
( ) 9. farmland	i. an area of low land between hills or mountains, often with a river flowing through it
( ) 10. forecast	j. one of the large land masses of the earth such as Europe, Asia or Africa
( ) 11. space	k. the time when the sun first appears in the sky in the morning
( ) 12. desert	l. the loud noise that you hear after a flash of lightning, during a storm
( ) 13. climate	m. a large area of land that has very little water and very few plants growing on it
( ) 14. coast	n. a place where a stream or river falls from a high place
( ) 15. freeze	o. a large ball of burning gas in space that we see as a point of light in the sky at night
( ) 16. humid	p. the area outside the earth's atmosphere where all the other planets and stars are
( ) 17. sunrise	q. an area of tropical forest where trees and plants grow very thickly
( ) 18. star	r. to become hard, and often turn to ice, as a result of extreme cold

✓ *MULTIPLE CHOICES*

(   ) 1. Between July and September, Beijing can have daytime temperatures of up to forty degrees *centigrade*.

     A. Celsius   B. Fahrenheit   C. centimeter

(   ) 2. Jessica's *hot* temper makes it really difficult for others to work with her.

     A. warm   B. spicy   C. fiery

(   ) 3. Until 1850, this place still remained to be *a cultural desert*.

     A. a place without any culture

     B. a place covered with lots of sand

     C. a place with little water

(   ) 4. We still have one guest standing here, so can you make *space* for an extra chair?

     A. separation   B. room   C. distance

(   ) 5. Temperatures are *forecast* to reach 40°C this Sunday in South China.

     A. claimed   B. predicted   C. broadcast

(   ) 6. Walking along the river, you can see *bushes* grow down to the water's edge.

     A. extremely tall trees   B. thick and low plants   C. plants as same as trees

(   ) 7. While they were quarreling, the car rolled over the edge of a *cliff*.

     A. low land   B. steep rock   C. ground under the sea

(   ) 8. I was attracted by the great *mountain range* of the Alps.

     A. steep cliff   B. solid rock   C. group of mountains

(   ) 9. These plants will grow best in a *humid* atmosphere.

     A. dry and hot   B. cold and wet   C. warm and damp

(   ) 10. There was a small *stream* at the end of the garden.

     A. a large wide river   B. a small narrow river   C. a small wide river

(   ) 11. This group of people live in a remote *island* off the coast of Scotland.

     A. land partially surrounded by water

     B. land completely surrounded by water

     C. land beside the sea or ocean

(   ) 12. The boy *growing* in a poor family becomes the president of his country, which inspires thousands of poor children to struggle for their dreams.

     A. being brought up   B. increasing   C. rising

(   ) 13. When you drive along the national highway, you can enjoy woods and fields that are typical features of the English *landscape*.

    A. sightseeing   B. scenery   C. picture

(   ) 14. We have spent the *mildest* winter since records began.

    A. hottest   B. coldest   C. most pleasant

(   ) 15. One of the most comfortable things must be enjoying a cool summer *breeze*.

    A. gentle sunshine   B. light rain   C. gentle wind

☑ FILLING THE BLANKS

climate;	degrees;	plant;	forest;	coast;
lightning;	branches;	blown;	planets;	grass;
countryside;	stormy;	fog;	wool;	beach

1. People destroy thousands of hectares of _____ each year to make paper.

2. We walked across the springy and soft _____ and decided to put up a tent there.

3. If you want to admire beautiful flowers, you need to water each _____ as often as required.

4. I like to live in the _____ for its peacefulness.

5. _____ is the very bright flashes of light in the sky that happen during thunderstorms.

6. Dense _____ is affecting roads in the north and visibility is poor.

7. The murder happened on a night of _____ weather, with torrential rain and high winds.

8. Jasmine bought a scarf of 100% _____ which cost 2,000 yuan.

9. Some of the tourists are sunbathing on the _____ while others are swimming in the sea.

10. Humans are faced with the threat of global _____ change, and we must join hands to make some effort.

11. Water boils at 100 _____ centigrade.

12. We will cut away the dead _____ from the trees.

13. Xiamen, located on the southeastern _____ of China, is known as 'a garden on the ocean'.

14. The wind was so heavy that the ship was _____ onto the rocks.

15. This picture shows the nine _____ in the solar system.

 **WRITING**

Write your answer in about 100 words.

You see this announcement on an English website for students.

Articles wanted!

Do you think it is important to protect endangered wild animals?

What are the physical difficulties in protecting endangered wild animals?

Does it cost a lot?

The best articles answering these questions will be published next month.

Write your article.

 # CHECK

1. desert _____   2. forest _____   3. island _____

4. 植物 _____   5. 太空；空间 _____   6. 湖泊 _____

7. world _____   8. field _____   9. wool _____

10. 树枝 _____   11. 微风 _____   12. 洞穴 _____

13. coast _____   14. centigrade _____   15. freeze _____

16. 山谷 _____   17. 瀑布 _____   18. rainforest _____

19. jungle _____   20. scenery _____

Day **16** *Animals* 动物世界

 VOCABULARY

✅ 基础词汇

词汇	词义		默写
bat /bæt/	n.	蝙蝠	
bear /beə(r)/	n.	熊	
bee /biː/	n.	蜜蜂	
bird /bɜːd/	n.	鸟	
chicken /ˈtʃɪkɪn/	n.	鸡	
cow /kaʊ/	n.	奶牛	
dolphin /ˈdɒlfɪn/	n.	海豚	
elephant /ˈelɪfənt/	n.	象	
fish /fɪʃ/	n.	鱼	
fur /fɜː(r)/	n.	毛皮	
horse /hɔːs/	n.	马	
lamb /læm/	n.	羔羊	
lion /ˈlaɪən/	n.	狮子	
monkey /ˈmʌnki/	n.	猴子	
mouse /maʊs/	n.	老鼠	
pet /pet/	n.	宠物	
pig /pɪg/	n.	猪	
rabbit /ˈræbɪt/	n.	兔	
snake /sneɪk/	n.	蛇	
sheep /ʃiːp/	n.	羊	
tiger /ˈtaɪgə(r)/	n.	老虎	
whale /weɪl/	n.	鲸	

✅ 重点词汇

词汇		词义	默写
bark /bɑːk/	v.	（狗）吠叫	
beetle /ˈbiːtl/	n.	甲虫	
bull /bʊl/	n.	公牛	
butterfly /ˈbʌtəflaɪ/	n.	蝴蝶	
dinosaur /ˈdaɪnəsɔː(r)/	n.	恐龙	
donkey /ˈdɒŋki/	n.	驴	
frog /frɒg/	n.	青蛙	
giraffe /dʒəˈrɑːf/	n.	长颈鹿	
goat /gəʊt/	n.	山羊	
herd /hɜːd/	n.	兽群；牧群	
insect /ˈɪnsekt/	n.	昆虫	
kangaroo /ˌkæŋgəˈruː/	n.	袋鼠	
kitten /ˈkɪtn/	n.	小猫	
mosquito /məˈskiːtəʊ/	n.	蚊子	
parrot /ˈpærət/	n.	鹦鹉	
polar bear	n.	北极熊	
penguin /ˈpeŋgwɪn/	n.	企鹅	
shark /ʃɑːk/	n.	鲨鱼	
sea creatures	n.	海洋生物	
species /ˈspiːʃiːz/	n.	种；物种	
tail /teɪl/	n.	尾巴	
turkey /ˈtɜːki/	n.	火鸡	
wolf /wʊlf/	n.	狼	
wing /wɪŋ/	n.	翅膀	
wildlife /ˈwaɪldlaɪf/	n.	野生动物	
zebra /ˈzebrə/	n.	斑马	

✅ 进阶加油站

◆ 与动物相关的谚语

Never offer to teach fish to swim.	不要班门弄斧。
Fine feathers make fine birds.	人靠衣装马靠鞍。
birds of a feather (flock together)	物以类聚
rain cats and dogs	倾盆大雨
let the cat out of the bag	（无意中）泄露秘密
like a cat on hot bricks	像热锅上的蚂蚁；局促不安；如坐针毡
have a frog in your throat	（暂时）失音，嗓音沙哑
make a monkey out of sb.	捉弄某人
let sleeping dogs lie	过去的事就不要再提了；不要没事找事
a lion in the way	拦路虎
a bull in a china shop	笨拙莽撞的人；冒失鬼

◆ 常用量词表达

- ***a herd of*** 一群（大的动物群体）

  eg. a herd of elephants/cows/horses/deer 一群象 / 牛 / 马 / 鹿

- ***a flock of*** 一群（羊，鸟等）

  eg. a flock of birds/sheep/goats/geese 一群鸟 / 绵羊 / 山羊 / 鹅

- ***a school of*** 一群（水生动物）

  eg. a school of fish/dolphins 一群鱼 / 海豚

◆ 单复数同形

- sheep 羊；绵羊

  eg. a sheep 一只羊   three sheep 三只羊

- deer 鹿

  eg. a deer 一头鹿   three deer 三头鹿

- fish 鱼

  eg. a fish 一条鱼   three fish 三条鱼

（当表示鱼的种类时，**fish** 后可加 **-es**。eg. many kinds of fishes 多种多样的鱼）

EXERCISE

✅ MATCH

( ) 1. fur

( ) 2. giraffe

( ) 3. bark

( ) 4. wildlife

( ) 5. mosquito

( ) 6. parrot

( ) 7. butterfly

( ) 8. penguin

( ) 9. dolphin

( ) 10. species

( ) 11. wolf

( ) 12. lamb

( ) 13. zebra

( ) 14. kitten

( ) 15. goat

( ) 16. bull

( ) 17. wing

( ) 18. frog

a. a flying insect that bites humans and animals and sucks their blood

b. a young cat

c. an animal with horns and a coat of hair, that lives wild in mountain areas or is kept on farms for its milk or meat

d. When a dog barks, it makes a short loud sound

e. one of the parts of the body of a bird, insect or bat that it uses for flying

f. a group into which animals, plants, etc. that are able to breed with each other

g. a small animal with smooth skin, that lives both on land and in water

h. a tall African animal with a very long neck, long legs, and dark marks on its coat

i. a flying insect with a long thin body and four large, usually brightly coloured, wings

j. animals, birds, insects, etc. that are wild and live in a natural environment

k. a black and white bird that lives in the Antarctic

l. a tropical bird with a curved beak and is kept as pets and can be trained to copy human speech

m. a young sheep

n. a large wild animal of the dog family, that lives and hunts in groups

o. the soft thick mass of hair that grows on the body of some animals

p. the male of any animal in the cow family

q. a sea animal that looks like a large fish with a pointed mouth

r. an African wild animal like a horse with black and white lines on its body

✓ MULTIPLE CHOICES

(   ) 1. When you see a person who acts in a rough way in a place where skill and care are needed, you will say he is like a_____in a china shop.

    A. zebra   B. dinosaur   C. bull

(   ) 2. When you are unable to speak clearly for a short time, you may tell your friends that you have a_____in your throat.

    A. insect   B. frog   C. parrot

(   ) 3 This is an important news, so I hope no one will let the_____out of the bag.

    A. dog   B. cat   C. wolf

(   ) 4. Which one is the right plural form of the word 'sheep'?

    A. sheep   B. sheeps   C. sheepes

(   ) 5. Which one is the right plural form of the word 'mouse'?

    A. mouse   B. mices   C. mice

(   ) 6. Which one is the right plural form of the word 'wolf'?

    A. wolf   B. wolfs   C. wolves

(   ) 7. What is the right name for 'a male animal of the cow family'?

    A. cow   B. bull   C. buffalo

(   ) 8. What is the right name for 'young cat'?

    A. kitten   B. puppy   C. calf

(   ) 9. In autumn, we sometimes can see a_____of wild geese flying overhead.

    A. herd   B. school   C. flock

(   ) 10. A_____of fish are swimming in the clear river.

    A. herd   B. school   C. flock

✓ FILLING THE BLANKS

tail;	fur;	shark;	dinosaurs;	turkey;
polar bears;	wildlife;	pets;	snake;	parrots;
species;	barking;	monkey;	mosquito;	wings

1. This rabbit's _____ is short, dense and silky.

2. I don't think it is a good idea to keep turtles as _____.

3. I was scared to death by a _____ coiling up in the grass.

4. That dog suddenly started _____ at us, which made us scared.

5. When an infected _____ bites a human, viruses are injected into the blood.

6. There are lots of animals in the North Pole, for example, whales, _____, and sea dogs.

7. _____ are so smart that they can mimic humans' voice.

8. _____ lived millions of years ago but is now extinct.

9. She was sad because some classmates made a _____ out of her.

10. The dog ran towards its master, wagging its _____.

11. He is exactly a _____ and gives bad advice to me to pay too much for that coat.

12. They will sit down to a traditional _____ dinner to celebrate the Thanksgiving Day.

13. It is necessary for the government to reconsider the project because the development of the area would endanger _____.

14. As we all know, pandas are an endangered _____.

15. The plane dipped its _____, circled back, then landed at the airport.

☑ LISTENING

You are going to hear people talking about two different situations. For each question, choose the correct answer.

1. You will hear part of a children's television programme about zebras.

   What does the presenter say about their appearance?

   A. All members of a family of zebras have the same stripes.

   B. Zebras can recognise each other by their stripes.

   C. Male and female Zebras have similar stripes.

扫码听录音

2. You will overhear a conversation between a boy and a girl about birds in the boy's garden.

   How does the boy's mother feel about birds?

   A. She enjoys watching them.

   B. She likes feeding them.

   C. She worries about them.

CHECK

1. cow _____

2. bull _____

3. fur _____

4. 蝙蝠 _____

5. 海豚 _____

6. 长颈鹿 _____

7. pet _____

8. rabbit _____

9. snake _____

10. 鲸鱼 _____

11. 大象 _____

12. 狮子 _____

13. beetle _____

14. frog _____

15. kangaroo _____

16. 蝴蝶 _____

17. 企鹅 _____

18. 北极熊 _____

19. turkey _____

20. zebra _____

Day ⑰ Town and City 城镇与城市

VOCABULARY

✓ 基础词汇

词汇		词义	默写
airport /ˈeəpɔːt/	*n.*	机场	
bar /bɑː(r)/	*n.*	酒吧	
bookshop /ˈbʊkʃɒp/	*n.*	书店	
bridge /brɪdʒ/	*n.*	桥	
car park	*n.*	停车场	
city centre	*n.*	市中心	
coffee shop	*n.*	小咖啡厅	
corner /ˈkɔːnə(r)/	*n.*	角；街角；墙角	
crowded /ˈkraʊdɪd/	*adj.*	充满的；拥挤的	
dirty /ˈdɜːti/	*adj.*	肮脏的	
market /ˈmɑːkɪt/	*n.*	集市；市场	
motorway /ˈməʊtəweɪ/	*n.*	高速公路	
noise /nɔɪz/	*n.*	噪音	
noisy /ˈnɔɪzi/	*adj.*	嘈杂的	
park /pɑːk/	*n.*	公园	
petrol station	*n.*	汽车加油站	
playground /ˈpleɪɡraʊnd/	*n.*	操场；游乐场	
quiet /ˈkwaɪət/	*adj.*	安静的	

roundabout /ˈraʊndəbaʊt/	*n.*	（交通）环岛
shopping centre	*n.*	购物中心
town /taʊn/	*n.*	市镇；城镇
zoo /zuː/	*n.*	动物园

☑ 重点词汇

词 汇		词 义	默写
booking office	*n.*	售票处	
cafeteria /ˌkæfəˈtɪəriə/	*n.*	自助餐厅	
cash machine	*n.*	自动取款机	
cashpoint /ˈkæʃpɔɪnt/	*n.*	自动取款机	
castle /ˈkɑːsl/	*n.*	城堡	
clinic /ˈklɪnɪk/	*n.*	诊所	
college /ˈkɒlɪdʒ/	*n.*	学院	
cottage /ˈkɒtɪdʒ/	*n.*	小屋；村舍；小别墅	
entrance /ˈentrəns/	*n.*	入口（处）	
fountain /ˈfaʊntən/	*n.*	喷泉	
gallery /ˈgæləri/	*n.*	画廊	
garage /ˈgærɑːdʒ/	*n.*	车库；汽车修理厂	
grocery (store)	*n.*	食品杂货店	
guest house	*n.*	小旅馆	
library /ˈlaɪbrəri/	*n.*	图书馆	
mall /mɔːl/	*n.*	购物商场	
monument /ˈmɒnjumənt/	*n.*	纪念碑	
museum /mjuˈziːəm/	*n.*	博物馆	
pavement /ˈpeɪvmənt/	*n.*	路面；人行道	

palace /ˈpæləs/	*n.*	宫殿
pharmacy /ˈfɑːməsi/	*n.*	药房
prison /ˈprɪzn/	*n.*	监狱
route /ruːt/	*n.*	路线；常规路线
ruin /ˈruːɪn/	*n.*	废墟；祸根；毁坏
	v.	毁坏；毁灭
signpost /ˈsaɪnpəʊst/	*n.*	路标
stadium /ˈsteɪdiəm/	*n.*	体育场
square /skweə(r)/	*n.*	广场
theatre /ˈθɪətə(r)/	*n.*	戏院；剧场；电影院
tunnel /ˈtʌnl/	*n.*	隧道
turning /ˈtɜːnɪŋ/	*n.*	转弯处

✅ 进阶加油站

◆ 词汇辨析

cafe, cafeteria, canteen

cafe：咖啡馆，小餐馆（供应饮料和便餐，在英美国家通常不供应酒类）

a place where you can buy drinks and simple meals. Alcohol is not usually served in British or American cafes

cafeteria：（医院、高校、商场等的）自助餐厅，食堂

a restaurant where you choose and pay for your meal at a counter and carry it to a table. Cafeterias are often found in factories, colleges, hospitals, etc.

cantee：食堂；餐厅

a place where food and drink are served in a factory, a school, etc.

EXERCISE

✓ MATCH

(   ) 1. roundabout

(   ) 2. motorway

(   ) 3. market

(   ) 4. bar

(   ) 5. noisy

(   ) 6. corner

(   ) 7. square

(   ) 8. bookshop

(   ) 9. airport

(   ) 10. crowded

(   ) 11. monument

(   ) 12. stadium

(   ) 13. route

(   ) 14. guest house

(   ) 15. turning

(   ) 16. college

(   ) 17. pavement

(   ) 18. signpost

(   ) 19. cottage

(   ) 20. tunnel

a. an open area in a town, usually with four sides, surrounded by buildings

b. having a lot of people or too many people

c. a place where students go to study or to receive training after they have left school

d. a large sports ground surrounded by rows of seats and usually other buildings

e. a wide road, with at least two lanes in each direction, where traffic can travel fast for long distances between large towns

f. a sign at the side of a road giving information about the direction and distance of places

g. a place where a road leads away from the one you are travelling on

h. making a lot of noise

i. a building, column, statue, etc. built to remind people of a famous person or event

j. a passage built underground, for example to allow a road or railway/railroad to go through a hill, under a river, etc.

k. a part of sth. where two or more sides, lines or edges join

l. a place where two or more roads meet, forming a circle that all traffic must go around in the same direction

m. a small house, especially in the country

n. a place where planes land and take off and that has buildings for passengers to wait in

o. the surface of a road

p. an occasion when people buy and sell goods

q. a small house built near a large house, for guests to stay in

r. a shop/store that sells books

s. a way that you follow to get from one place to another

t. a place where you can buy and drink alcoholic and other drinks

☑ *MULTIPLE CHOICES*

(   ) 1. Jessie always takes her car to *a local garage* for a check-up every month.

    A. a place where the car can be repaired

    B. a place which sells cars

    C. a place where the car can be washed

(   ) 2. They used to own a charming *cottage* with roses around the door.

    A. a building with glass sides and a glass roof for growing plants in

    B. a small house, especially in the country

    C. a small simple building, usually built of wood or metal, used for keeping things in

(   ) 3. She flicked a crumb(面包屑) off the *corner* of her mouth and walked into the classroom.

    A. end   B. lip   C. side

(   ) 4. He was sent to *prison* for fifteen years because he had killed two innocent people.

    A. a locked house   B. police station   C. jail

(   ) 5. Gambling was his *ruin* and he lost his reputation as well as families due to it.

    A. downfall   B. success   C. harm

(   ) 6. After snowing for the whole night, you could find cars skidded on the icy *pavement*.

    A. motorway   B. highway   C. road surface

(   ) 7. Sunny had an overpriced beef steak in the hotel *cafeteria*.

    A. cafe   B. restaurant   C. bakery

(   ) 8. It is really easy to find a nearby Wal-Mart. Just follow the *signposts*.

    A. road signs   B. traffic lights   C. signal boxes

(   ) 9. A *monument* to Duke of Wellington was erected in St Paul's Cathedral.

    A. moment   B. memory   C. memorial

(   ) 10. This is the most direct way to the *mall*.

    A.market   B.square   C.shopping centre

(   ) 11. That seven-year-old boy in red playing in the *playground* is my son.

    A. indoor gymnasium   B. schoolyard   C. soccer field

(   ) 12. We entered a room *crowded* with books and saw that man.

    A. filled   B. empty   C. bare

(   ) 13. The local *theatre* averagely shows seven movies a week.

       A. opera house   B. cinema   C. grand hall

(   ) 14. The house is not on a bus *route*, so you have to walk 0.5 mile to catch a bus.

       A. fixed way   B. channel   C. passage

☑ FILLING THE BLANKS

dirty;	pharmacy;	corner;	palace;	college;
gallery;	tunnel;	clinic;	crowded;	museum;
pavement;	prison;	entrance;	ruins;	signpost

1. Zhang Guifang, a 24-year-old _____ graduate, made a bold decision to return to her village in Henan province.

2. They drove a _____ through the solid rock, which linked Hunan province and Hubei province.

3. Pick up the medicine from the _____ and take it after you eat dinner for thirty minutes.

4. Joey is being treated at the local _____ and she feels much better now.

5. The famous painting is in the _____ upstairs.

6. The National _____ of China houses more than 1.4 million items of collection, covering ancient and modern artifacts, books, and works of art.

7. The Summer _____, Tiantan Park and Beijing Zoo were reported as the most popular destinations during the three-day Dragon Boat Festival holiday.

8. Two men were walking briskly down the _____ towards Jimmy.

9. I did not like the woman because her fingernails were always _____.

10. There is a cabinet in the _____ of the room.

11. The police put the thief in _____.

12. A large number of churches fell into _____ after the civil war.

13. We have a very _____ schedule and have no time to walk around the city.

14. Tomorrow, I will meet you at the _____ of the shopping mall.

15. The _____ on the side of the road tells us where the two paths converged.

 **LISTENING**

Questions 1-3
For each question, choose the correct answer.

1. Where is the cycling race going to finish?

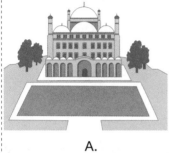
A.

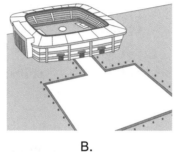
B.

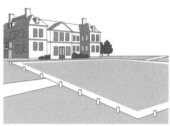
C.

2. Where will the tourist go tomorrow?

A.

B.

C.

3. Where will they have something to eat?

A.

B.

C.

CHECK

1. bar _____

2. bookshop _____

3. bridge _____

4. 机场 _____

5. 市场 _____

6. 街角 _____

7. crowded _____

8. noise _____

9. square _____

10. 城堡 _____

11. 小屋 _____

12. 喷泉 _____

13. route _____

14. gallery _____

15. museum _____

16. 纪念碑 _____

17. 宫殿 _____

18. 监狱 _____

19. pharmacy _____

20. stadium _____

Day 18 Environment 环境

VOCABULARY

✅ 基础词汇

词　汇	词　义		默写
clean /kliːn/	*adj.*	干净的	
dirty /ˈdɜːti/	*adj.*	肮脏的	
environment /ɪnˈvaɪrənmənt/	*n.*	环境	
environmental /ɪnˌvaɪrənˈmentl/	*adj.*	环境的	
electricity /ɪˌlekˈtrɪsəti/	*n.*	电	
metal /ˈmetl/	*n.*	金属	
nature /ˈneɪtʃə(r)/	*n.*	自然界；自然	
oil /ɔɪl/	*n.*	油	
paper /ˈpeɪpə(r)/	*n.*	纸张	
petrol /ˈpetrəl/	*n.*	汽油	
plant /plɑːnt/	*n.*	植物	
plastic /ˈplæstɪk/	*n.*	塑料	
rubbish /ˈrʌbɪʃ/	*n.*	垃圾	
waste /weɪst/	*n.*	浪费	

✓ 重点词汇

词 汇		词 义	默写
coal /kəʊl/	*n.*	煤	
endangered /ɪnˈdeɪndʒəd/	*adj.*	濒危的	
energy /ˈenədʒi/	*n.*	能源	
exhausted /ɪgˈzɔːstɪd/	*adj.*	用完的；耗尽的	
fuel /ˈfjuːəl/	*n.*	燃料	
global /ˈgləʊbl/	*adj.*	全球的	
hunting /ˈhʌntɪŋ/	*n.*	打猎；狩猎	
litter /ˈlɪtə(r)/	*n.*	垃圾	
planet /ˈplænɪt/	*n.*	行星	
poison /ˈpɔɪzn/	*n.*	毒素；毒药	
poisonous /ˈpɔɪzənəs/	*adj.*	有毒的	
pollution /pəˈluːʃn/	*n.*	污染	
pollut /pəˈluːt/	*v.*	污染	
prohibit /prəˈhɪbɪt/	*v.*	禁止	
protect /prəˈtekt/	*v.*	保护	
protection /prəˈtekʃn/	*n.*	保护	
punish /ˈpʌnɪʃ/	*v.*	惩罚	
punishment /ˈpʌnɪʃmənt/	*n.*	惩罚	
recycle /ˌriːˈsaɪkl/	*v.*	回收利用	
recycling /riːˈsaɪklɪŋ/	*n.*	回收利用	
rescue /ˈreskjuː/	*v.*	营救	
resource /rɪˈsɔːs/	*n.*	资源	
shortage /ˈʃɔːtɪdʒ/	*n.*	短缺	
species /ˈspiːʃiːz/	*n.*	物种	
tin /tɪn/	*n.*	罐	
universe /ˈjuːnɪvɜːs/	*n.*	宇宙	
universal /ˌjuːnɪˈvɜːsl/	*adj.*	普遍的	
variety /vəˈraɪəti/	*n.*	变化；多样性；品种	
warning /ˈwɔːnɪŋ/	*n.*	警告	

进阶加油站

◆ 高频短语

bottle bank	玻璃瓶回收箱	climate change	气候变化
global warming	全球变暖	natural resources	自然资源
recycling resources	可再生资源	illegal hunting	非法狩猎
endangered species	濒危物种	environmentally-friendly	环境友好型的
environment pollution	环境污染	low-carbon	低碳的

EXERCISE

MATCH

( ) 1. variety

( ) 2. petrol

( ) 3. pollution

( ) 4. energy

( ) 5. protection

( ) 6. fuel

( ) 7. paper

( ) 8. environment

( ) 9. shortage

( ) 10. climate

a. the thin material that you write and draw on and that is also used for wrapping and packing things

b. the process of making air, water, soil, etc. dirty

c. a situation when there is not enough of the people or things that are needed

d. a source of power, such as fuel, used for driving machines, providing heat, etc.

e. several different sorts of the same thing

f. the act of protecting sb./sth.

g. any material that produces heat or power, usually when it is burnt

h. a liquid obtained from petroleum, used as fuel in car engines, etc.

i. the regular pattern of weather conditions of a particular place

j. the natural world in which people, animals and plants live

✅ MULTIPLE CHOICES

(   ) 1. Agreement on the issue of teenager protection is almost *universal*.

     A. typical   B. common   C. particular

(   ) 2. *There is no shortage of* things to do in the town centre.

     A. There are plenty of

     B. There is a lack of

     C. There is a shortness of

(   ) 3. The authorities have warned the citizens not to bathe in the *polluted* river.

     A. clean   B. broken   C. contaminated

(   ) 4. I don't believe that Henry will *punish the children* for such minor mistakes.

     A. make the children suffer

     B. forgive the children

     C. release the children

(   ) 5. Supplies of food will be *exhausted* within three days.

     A. sufficient   B. eaten up   C. lost

(   ) 6. The new regulation says anyone who drop *litter* will be fined.

     A. rubbish   B. plastic bags   C. poison

(   ) 7. During the outbreak of the COVID-19, each company is trying it's best to *protect* its own commercial interests and survive in the serious situation.

     A. object   B. preserve   C. protest

(   ) 8. I hate to see good food *go to waste*, so I always try to eat the food all.

     A. be thrown away   B. be recycled   C. go bad

(   ) 9. Tobacco advertising in newspapers and magazines is *prohibited* in that country.

     A. protected   B. allowed   C. forbidden

(   ) 10. We all need *variety* in our diet to keep fit.

     A. kind   B. diversity   C. multiples

(   ) 11. Mike got off with a *caution* as he was a first offender.

     A. care   B. strictness   C. warning

(   ) 12. You should be careful in the forest, because some mushrooms contain a deadly *poison*.

A. poisonous substance

B. a sleeping substance

C. a poisonous pill

(   ) 13. This is an *environmentally sensitive* area which needs our special protection.

    A. easily damaged   B. very subtle   C. various

(   ) 14. It becomes illegal for otter *hunting* since 1977.

    A. searching   B. chasing and killing   C. cooking

✓ FILLING THE BLANKS

universe;   environment;   metal;   pollution;   electricity;
endangered;   plants;   recycle;   punishment;   paper;
poisonous;   plastic;   climate;   petrol;   shortage

1. According to a recent research, home _____ can affect a child's behaviour.

2. Last year, the Browns moved into a cabin with _____ but no running water.

3. All _____ need enough light and water to grow better.

4. A lot of _____ bags which cannot be recycled have caused severe white pollution.

5. With the rapid rise in prices for oil and _____, many car owners choose to buy electric cars.

6. She wrote the guest's name and address on a slip of _____ last night.

7. You should be careful that the leaves of certain trees are _____ to cattle.

8. The government has set a series of regulations to reduce levels of environmental _____.

9. Einstein's equations（爱因斯坦的方程式）show that the _____ is always expanding.

10. We have bought pieces of furniture in wood, _____, and glass.

11. It will build more wild animal captive breeding centres and help those _____ wild animals under captive breeding, such as the giant panda, milu deer and crested ibis（朱鹮）, return to the wild.

12. We are going to _____ 98 percent of domestic waste by the end of this year.

13. During the war time, many families can't feed themselves adequately because of the

_____ of food.

14. We should join our hands to cope with the threat of global _____ change.

15. He was sent to prison as a _____ of murdering a witness.

☑ WRITING

Write your answer in about **100 words**.
You see this announcement on an English-language website.

Articles wanted!

Do you think environment protection is important?
What are the main causes to environment pollution?
What's your suggestion for environment protection?
The best articles answering these questions will win a prize.
Write your article.

CHECK

1. dirty _____

2. rubbish _____

3. petrol _____

4. 金属 _____

5. 环境 _____

6. 塑料 _____

7. nature _____

8. waste _____

9. electricity _____

10. 濒危的 _____

11. 耗尽的 _____

12. 有毒的 _____

13. pollution _____

14. protection _____

15. rescue _____

16. 资源 _____

17. 警告 _____

18. 品种 _____

19. coal _____

20. prohibit _____

Day ⑲ *Time and Units* 时间与单位

VOCABULARY

☑ 基础词汇

词 汇	词 义	默写
January /ˈdʒænjuəri/	n.　一月	
February /ˈfebruəri/	n.　二月	
March /mɑːtʃ/	n.　三月	
April /ˈeɪprəl/	n.　四月	
May /meɪ/	n.　五月	
June /dʒuːn/	n.　六月	
July /dʒuˈlaɪ/	n.　七月	
August /ˈɔːgəst/	n.　八月	
September /sepˈtembə(r)/	n.　九月	
October /ɒkˈtəʊbə(r)/	n.　十月	
November /nəʊˈvembə(r)/	n.　十一月	
December /dɪˈsembə(r)/	n.　十二月	
Monday /ˈmʌndeɪ/	n.　星期一	
Tuesday /ˈtjuːzdeɪ/	n.　星期二	
Wednesday /ˈwenzdeɪ/	n.　星期三	
Thursday /ˈθɜːzdeɪ/	n.　星期四	
Friday /ˈfraɪdeɪ/	n.　星期五	
Saturday /ˈsætədeɪ/	n.　星期六	
Sunday /ˈsʌndeɪ/	n.　星期日	

hour /ˈaʊə(r)/	*n.*	小时
hundred /ˈhʌndrəd/	*n.*	一百
minute /ˈmɪnɪt/	*n.*	分钟
midday /ˌmɪdˈdeɪ/	*n.*	正午
midnight /ˈmɪdnaɪt/	*n.*	午夜
quarter /ˈkwɔːtə(r)/	*n.*	一刻钟
second /ˈsekənd/	*n.*	秒
thousand /ˈθaʊznd/	*n.*	一千
tonight /təˈnaɪt/	*adv.*	在今晚
weekday /ˈwiːkdeɪ/	*n.*	周工作日
weekend /ˌwiːkˈend/	*n.*	周末；星期六和星期日

✅ 重点词汇

词 汇	词 义		默 写
bedtime /ˈbedtaɪm/	*n.*	睡觉时间	
billion /ˈbɪljən/	*n.*	十亿	
century /ˈsentʃəri/	*n.*	世纪	
day off	*n.*	休假日	
dynasty /ˈdɪnəsti/	*n.*	朝代	
gram /græm/	*n.*	克	
kilogram /ˈkɪləgræm/	*n.*	千克	
kilometre /ˈkɪləmiːtə(r)/	*n.*	千米	
length /leŋθ/	*n.*	长度	
lunchtime /ˈlʌntʃtaɪm/	*n.*	午餐时间	
metre /ˈmiːtə(r)/	*n.*	米	
million /ˈmɪljən/	*n.*	一百万	
mile /maɪl/	*n.*	英里	
ton /tʌn/	*n.*	吨	
trillion /ˈtrɪljən/	*n.*	万亿	
width /wɪdθ/	*n.*	宽度	

✅ 进阶加油站

◆ 常用数词总结

one thousand 一千	one hundred million / 0.1 billion 一亿
ten thousand 一万	one billion 十亿
one hundred thousand / 0.1 million 十万	ten billion 一百亿
one million 一百万	one hundred billion / 0.1 trillion 一千亿
ten million 一千万	one trillion 一万亿

◆ 时间点的表达

- "钟点数 + o'clock"，意为"几时"。

  eg. one o'clock 1 时   ten o'clock 10 时

- "分钟数 +past+ 钟点数"，意为"几时过几分"。

  eg. twenty past three 3 时 20 分   ten past six 6 时 10 分

- "（60- 原分钟数）+ to +（原钟点数 +1）"，意为"差几分到几时"。

  eg. ten to nine 8 时 50 分   twenty to four 3 时 40 分

- half past ... ……30 分 / 半

  eg. half past six 6 时 30 分   half past ten 10 时 30 分

- quarter past... ……15 分 / 一刻

  eg. a quarter past eight 7 时 15 分   a quarter past two 2 时 15 分

- a.m.=in the morning，指午夜 12 时至正午 12 时前的时间。

  eg. 6 a.m. 早上 6 时   1 a.m. 凌晨 1 时

- p.m. =in the afternoon/evening or at night，指正午 12 时至午夜 12 时前的时间。

  eg. 8 p.m. 晚上 8 时   3 p.m. 下午 3 时

◆ 易混淆知识点

- hundred, thousand, million, billion 等词在表达具体的数量时，其后不加 -s；若前面没有具体的数量，其后要加 -s。

  eg. two hundred people 两百人   hundreds of people 数百人

      three thousand pounds 三千英镑   thousands of birds 成千上万的鸟

      four million books 四百万册书   millions of readers 数百万的读者

EXERCISE

✅ MATCH

( ) 1. March	a. a unit for measuring weight
( ) 2. million	b. 12 o'clock at night
( ) 3. century	c. the 8th month of the year
( ) 4. gram	d. 1,000,000
( ) 5. lunchtime	e. the 11th month of the year
( ) 6. weekend	f. the 3rd month of the year, between February and April
( ) 7. tonight	g. the 6th month of the year
( ) 8. Thursday	h. on or during the evening or night of today
( ) 9. Sunday	i. 12 o'clock in the middle of the day
( ) 10. midnight	j. Saturday and Sunday
( ) 11. November	k. a period of 15 minutes either before or after every hour
( ) 12. midday	l. a period of 100 years
( ) 13. August	m. the day of the week after Wednesday and before Friday
( ) 14. quarter	n. the day of the week after Saturday and before Monday
( ) 15. June	o. the time around the middle of the day when people usually eat lunch

✅ MULTIPLE CHOICES

( ) 1. Did you happen to see Mike leave last _Wednesday_?

    A. the day after Tuesday and before Thursday

    B. the day after Monday and before Thursday

    C. the day after Friday and before Sunday

(　　) 2. At *midday*, everyone would go down to that local restaurant.

  A. six day in the afternoon

  B. twelve o'clock at night

  C. twelve o'clock in the middle of the day

(　　) 3. It was *a quarter to six* when I saw that thief slipped into my neighbour's house.

  A. 5:45   B. 5:15   C. 6:15

(　　) 4. If you want to avoid the crowds, I suggest you to come on a *weekday*.

  A. Saturday and Sunday

  B. any of the days of the week except Saturday and Sunday

  C. any of the days of the week except Sunday

(　　) 5. It was Lily's *day off*, and Jason was on duty in her place.

  A. a day on which you do not have to work

  B. a working day on which you have to work

  C. a vacation when you can have a relax

(　　) 6. Jack, what are you doing? It's way past your *bedtime*!

  A. the time when sb. needs to get up

  B. the time when sb. needs to go to work

  C. the time when sb. usually goes to bed

(　　) 7. Up to *eight million* people a year visit China.

  A. 8,000,000   B. 80,000,000   C. 800,000,000

(　　) 8. That company has spent *billions* on a problem but it is still not resolved.

  A. more than 10,000,000

  B. more than 1,000,000

  C. more than 1,000,000,000

(　　) 9. That building covers an area of *80 square kilometres*.

  A. 80,000 square metres B. 1,000 metres C. 8,000 metres

(　　) 10. The first plane is due to leave on *May* 2nd.

  A. the third month of the year

  B. the fourth month of the year

  C. the fifth month of the year

✅ *FILLING THE BLANKS*

Monday;	**kilograms;**	**bedtime;**	**lunchtime;**	**hour;**
midnight;	**seconds;**	**century;**	**hundreds;**	**width**

1. I have bought a new car whose top speed is 120 miles per _____.

2. This vase is worth _____ of dollars.

3. Jane could run 100 metres in just over 11 _____.

4. The famous eighteenth _____ writers in Britain include Daniel Defoe, Jonathan Swift and Henry Fielding.

5. The road is reduced to 15 metres in _____ by adding parking bays.

6. I have received a parcel weighing around 4.5 _____.

7. The takeout still hadn't arrived by _____, so I phoned the deliveryman to figure out what had happened.

8. Did your parents read you _____ stories when you were a little girl?

9. We go and do the weekly shopping every _____ afternoon.

10. Jonathan was asleep after burning the _____ oil trying to finish his dissertation.

✅ *LISTENING*

Questions 1-2

For each question, choose the correct answer.

1. What time does the hiking begin?

扫码听录音

1:24pm	3:15pm	10:30am
A.	B.	C.

2. When does the girl plan to get up?

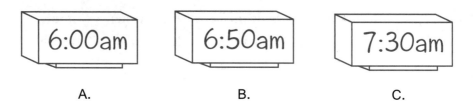

A.   B.   C.

CHECK

1. 一月 _____

2. 六月 _____

3. 七月 _____

4. Wednesday _____

5. Thursday _____

6. Tuesday _____

7. 周工作日 _____

8. 周末 _____

9. 星期日 _____

10. quarter _____

11. tonight _____

12. lunchtime _____

13. 世纪 _____

14. 朝代 _____

15. 千克 _____

16. kilometre _____

17. million _____

18. length _____

19. 吨 _____

20. 万亿 _____

Day ❷⓪ *Continents and Countries*
大陆与国家

VOCABULARY

 基础词汇

词 汇	词 义		默 写
Africa /ˈæfrɪkə/	*n.*	非洲	
America /əˈmerɪkə/	*n.*	美洲；美国	
Asia /ˈeɪʒə/	*n.*	亚洲	
Australia /ɒˈstreɪliə/	*n.*	澳大利亚	
Britain /ˈbrɪtn/	*n.*	英国	
Canada /ˈkænədə/	*n.*	加拿大	
China /ˈtʃaɪnə/	*n.*	中国	
Europe /ˈjʊərəp/	*n.*	欧洲	
France /frɑːns/	*n.*	法国	
Germany /ˈdʒɜːməni/	*n.*	德国	
Italy /ˈɪtəli/	*n.*	意大利	
Japan /dʒəˈpæn/	*n.*	日本	
North America	*n.*	北美洲	
South America	*n.*	南美洲	
Russia /ˈrʌʃə/	*n.*	俄罗斯	
Spain /speɪn/	*n.*	西班牙	

✅ 重点词汇

词汇		词义	默写
Antarctica /ænˈtɑːktɪkə/	n.	南极洲	
Arctic /ˈɑːktɪk/	n.	北极；北极地区	
Austria /ˈɒstriə/	n.	奥地利	
Brazil /brəˈzɪl/	n.	巴西	
Denmark /ˈdenmɑːk/	n.	丹麦	
Egypt /ˈiːdʒɪpt/	n.	埃及	
Greece /griːs/	n.	希腊	
India /ˈɪndiə/	n.	印度	
Mexico /ˈmeksɪkəʊ/	n.	墨西哥	
North Korea	n.	朝鲜	
Norway /ˈnɔːweɪ/	n.	挪威	
Oceania /ˌəʊsiˈɑːniə/	n.	大洋洲	
Poland /ˈpəʊlənd/	n.	波兰	
Portugal /ˈpɔːtʃʊgl/	n.	葡萄牙	
South Korea	n.	韩国	
Sweden /ˈswiːdn/	n.	瑞典	
Sydney /ˈsɪdni/	n.	悉尼	
Thailand /ˈtaɪlænd/	n.	泰国	
(the) Netherlands	n.	荷兰	
Turkey /ˈtɜːki/	n.	土耳其	

✅ 进阶加油站

◆ 四大洋

the Pacific Ocean	太平洋	the Atlantic Ocean	大西洋
the India Ocean	印度洋	the Arctic Ocean	北冰洋

◆ "国家"的多种表达

中国 *China* *the People's Republic of China (PRC)*	荷兰 *Holland* （*the*）*Netherlands*
英国 *the Great Britain* *the United Kingdom (UK)*	美国 *America* *the United States (US)* *the United States of America (USA)*

EXERCISE

MATCH

(　) 1. the US	a. the regions of the world around the South Pole
(　) 2. the UK	b. the United Kingdom
(　) 3. the Pacific Ocean	c. the largest country in the world
(　) 4. Russia	d. the United States of America
(　) 5. Sydney	e. the largest ocean in the world
(　) 6. Antarctica	f. the second largest country in the world
(　) 7. Arctic	g. the largest continent
(　) 8. Canada	h. the regions of the world around the North Pole
(　) 9. Asia	i. the largest city of Australia
(　) 10. Spain	J. a country in south-western Europe

☑ *MULTIPLE CHOICES*

(   ) 1. Located in Tanzania, Mount Kilimanjaro（乞力马扎罗山）is the _____ continent's highest peak at 5,895 meters.

     A. European   B. African   C. Asian

(   ) 2. Last weekend, my family went to watch operas in the Sydney Opera House in _____.

     A. Spain   B. Austria   C. Australia

(   ) 3. Andersen, the famous _____ writer of fairy tales, has written some famous fairy tales such as *the Ugly Duckling*.

     A. Indian   B. Danish   C. Sweden

(   ) 4. The official language of _____ is Portuguese.

     A. South Korea   B. Brazil   C. Saudi Arabia

(   ) 5. The capital of _____ is Bangkok（曼谷）which is also an international city.

     A. Thailand   B. Korea   C. the Netherlands

(   ) 6. The Yangtze River is the longest river in _____ and the third longest in the world.

     A. China   B. Greece   C. Mexico

(   ) 7. The _____ pyramid（金字塔）is one of the seven wonders of the world.

     A. Canadian   B. Egyptian   C. Turkish

(   ) 8. Visiting the characteristic windmill（风车）of _____ is undoubtedly one of the highlights of the trip.

     A. Poland   B. America   C. the Netherlands

(   ) 9. Zeus（宙斯）is called the Lord of Olympia in _____ mythology.

     A. Portugal   B. France   C. Greek

(   ) 10. China, Japan, Thailand and India are all _____ countries.

     A. Asian   B. European   C. American

☑ *FILLING THE BLANKS*

South American;	Britain;	Italy;	North American;	European;
Germans;	Antarctica;	Spain;	India;	France

1. The euro is the common currency of some countries of the _____ Union.

2. Many scientists went to the _____ to observe emperor penguins.

3. _____ is the world's second most populous country after China, with a population of more than 1.3 billion.

4. Bullfighting is a traditional public entertainment in _____.

5. Paris, the capital of _____, is known as the City of Romance.

6. _____ are generally considered to be serious, conservative, introspective and cautious in doing business.

7. Rome, the capital and largest city of _____, is also the national political, economic, cultural and transportation centre.

8. Columbia, Brazil and Peru（秘鲁）are all _____ countries.

9. My cousin went to study in the University of Oxford in _____.

10. The USA, Canada and Mexico are all _____ countries.

☑ SPEAKING

1. **Tell me something about your favourite country.**

2. **Tell me something about your hometown.**

CHECK

1. 非洲 _____   2. 亚洲 _____   3. 欧洲 _____

4. Canada _____   5. Britain _____   6. France _____

7. 意大利 _____   8. 日本 _____   9. 俄罗斯 _____

10. Austria _____   11. Brazil _____   12. Denmark _____

13. 埃及 _____   14. 希腊 _____   15. 印度 _____

16. Norway _____   17. Poland _____   18. South Korea _____

19. 泰国 _____   20. 土耳其 _____

Day ㉑ *Languages* 语言

VOCABULARY

✅ 基础词汇

词 汇	词 义		默 写
Chinese /ˌtʃaɪˈniːz/	n.	中文	
English /ˈɪŋglɪʃ/	n.	英文	
French /frentʃ/	n.	法语	
German /ˈdʒɜːmən/	n.	德语	
Japanese /ˌdʒæpəˈniːz/	n.	日语	
Italian /ɪˈtæliən/	n.	意大利语	
Russian /ˈrʌʃn/	n.	俄语	
Spanish /ˈspænɪʃ/	n.	西班牙语	
chat /tʃæt/	v.	闲聊；聊天	
conversation /ˌkɒnvəˈseɪʃn/	n.	交谈；谈话	
grammar /ˈgræmə(r)/	n.	语法	
phrase /freɪz/	n.	短语	
pronounce /prəˈnaʊns/	v.	发音	
pronunciation /prəˌnʌnsiˈeɪʃn/	n.	发音	
speech /spiːtʃ/	n.	演说；讲话	
vocabulary /vəˈkæbjələri/	n.	词汇；词汇量	

✅ 重点词汇

词 汇	词 义	默写
alphabet /ˈælfəbet/	*n.*　字母表	
article /ˈɑːtɪkl/	*n.*　（报刊上的）文章	
Chinese character	*n.*　汉字	
context /ˈkɒntekst/	*n.*　语境	
Danish /ˈdeɪnɪʃ/	*n.*　丹麦语	
dialect /ˈdaɪəlekt/	*n.*　方言	
essay /ˈeseɪ/	*n.*　文章；论文	
fluent /ˈfluːənt/	*adj.*　流利的；流畅的	
fluency /ˈfluːənsi/	*n.*　流利；流畅	
formal language	*n.*　正式用语	
informal language	*n.*　非正式用语	
mother tongue	*n.*　母语	
native speaker	*n.*　母语使用者	
oral /ˈɔːrəl/	*adj.*　口头的	
poem /ˈpəʊɪm/	*n.*　诗	
poetry /ˈpəʊətri/	*n.*　诗歌；诗集	
Polish /ˈpəʊlɪʃ/	*n.*　波兰语	
prose /prəʊz/	*n.*　散文	
spelling /ˈspelɪŋ/	*n.*　拼写	
stress /stres/	*n.*　重音；重读	
structure /ˈstrʌktʃə(r)/	*n.*　结构	
Swedish /ˈswiːdɪʃ/	*n.*　瑞典语	

✓ 进阶加油站

◆ 国家，国籍与语言

国家	国籍	语言
China 中国	Chinese 中国人	Chinese 汉语
France 法国	French 法国人	French 法语
Japan 日本	Japanese 日本人	Japanese 日语
Germany 德国	German 德国人	German 德语
Italy 意大利	Italian 意大利人	Italian 意大利语
Russia 俄罗斯	Russian 俄罗斯人	Russian 俄语
Spain 西班牙	Spanish 西班牙人	Spanish 西班牙语

◆ 词汇辨析

dialect, accent

dialect: **方言；地方话**

eg. *It's difficult to understand the local dialect.* 当地的方言很难懂。

accent: **口音；腔调**

eg. *She spoke English with a strong Indian accent.* 她说英语带着浓重的印度口音。

EXERCISE

✓ MATCH

( ) 1. vocabulary	a. spoken rather than written
( ) 2. pronounce	b. belonging or relating to Russia, or to its people, language, or culture
( ) 3. Spanish	c. the act of forming words correctly from individual letters
( ) 4. grammar	d. of or connected with France, its people or its language
( ) 5. speech	e. a person who speaks a language as their first language and has not learned it as a foreign language
( ) 6. alphabet	f. all the words that a person knows or uses
( ) 7. oral	g. to make the sound of a word or letter in a particular way
( ) 8. spelling	h. the language of Denmark
( ) 9. article	i. a formal talk that a person gives to an audience
( ) 10. native speaker	j. the language of China
( ) 11. Russian	k. a set of letters or symbols in a fixed order used for writing a language
( ) 12. Danish	l. the language, originally of England, now spoken in many other countries and used as a language of international communication throughout the world
( ) 13. essay	m. the rules in a language for changing the form of words and joining them into sentences
( ) 14. mother tongue	n. a short piece of writing by a student as part of a course of study
( ) 15. phrase	o. the language of Spain and of most countries in Central and South America
( ) 16. Chinese	p. the language that you first learn to speak when you are a child
( ) 17. English	q. a group of words without a finite verb, especially one that forms part of a sentence
( ) 18. French	r. a piece of writing about a particular subject in a newspaper or magazine

☑ *MULTIPLE CHOICES*

(   ) 1. The president made the announcement in a _____ on TV.

     A. speech   B. sound   C. propaganda

(   ) 2. I find that very few of my American classmates can _____ my name correctly.

     A. declare   B. pronounce   C. claim

(   ) 3. I suggest you to read various kinds of books because it can help to increase

     your _____.

     A. vocabulary   B. words   C. grammar

(   ) 4. When using a dictionary, you can find the English _____ has 26 letters.

     A. pronunciation   B. alphabet   C. syllables

(   ) 5. There are hundreds of different _____ spoken by people in China.

     A. mother tongues   B. mandarins   C. dialects

(   ) 6. _____ in French is the basic requirement for this job.

     A. Capacity   B. Fluency   C. Usage

(   ) 7. Answers can be written or presented _____ on tape.

     A. orally   B. literally   C. wordily

(   ) 8. His writings include novels and _____.

     A. pose   B. prose   C. phrase

(   ) 9. There are some differences between British and American _____ like 'favourite'

     and 'favorite'.

     A. spelling   B. phrases   C. grammars

(   ) 10. She practiced oral English with _____ to make her pronunciation better.

     A. foreigners   B. learners   C. native speakers

☑ *FILLING THE BLANKS*

informal language;	vocabulary; fluent;	poem;
mother tongue;	grammar system;	stress;
essay;	pronunciation;	alphabet

1. Mary has studied four foreign languages but is _____ in only two of them.

2. In the final oral exam, the teacher found Leo still had a misplaced _____ on the first syllable of the last word.

3. The first step in learning a foreign language is to grasp the basic rules of _____.

4. A group of professors are trying to find out how children learn to speak their _____.

5. That famous journalist wrote an _____ on the causes of the First World War.

6. There is more than one _____ of 'desert'.

7. The brand Xinghuacun is actually named after a _____ written by Tang Dynasty poet Du Mu.

8. It's not suitable to use _____ in a formal international conference.

9. M comes between L and N in the English _____.

10. The word 'failure' is never in my _____.

✓ READING

Questions 1-6

For each question, choose the correct answer.

Language is a tool for thinking and 1 _____. As a child, you learn to think and communicate in your mother tongue 2 _____ and unconsicously. 3 _____, learning a second language is not an easy thing. Language is a set of commonly accepted signs and the structural relationships between these signs is a system of 4 _____. Of course it's hard to memorize the 5 _____, grammar rules and idioms of a foreign language, but the more difficult thing maybe is the 6 _____ influence of your mother tongue.

1. A. communicate	B. communication	C. intercommunication
2. A. hardly	B. effortly	C. effortlessly
3. A. Therefore	B. However	C. Consequently
4. A. grammar	B. vocabulary	C. pronunciation
5. A. alphabet	B. stress	C. vocabulary
6. A. positive	B. negative	C. effective

CHECK

1. 法语 _____   2. 德语 _____   3. 意大利语 _____

4. Spanish _____   5. Russian _____   6. pronunciation _____

7. 字母表 _____   8. 汉字 _____   9. 方言 _____

10. formal language _____   11. mother tongue _____

12. native speaker _____   13. 散文 _____

14. 诗集 _____   15. 重音 _____

16. article _____   17. Polish _____   18. Swedish _____

19. 流利的 _____   20. 拼写 _____